Notes Pocket Pal

An abridged version of the best seller:
Notes from the Grooming Table

by Melissa Verplank, CMG

with Illustrations by Lisa VanSweden

Published by:

WHITE DOG ENTERPRISES

White Dog Enterprises, Inc.
16060 Peach Ridge Avenue
Kent City, Michigan 49330

White Dog Enterprises educational materials may be purchased
in bulk for educational, business or sales promotional use.
For information, please write:

White Dog Enterprises, Inc.
16060 Peach Ridge Avenue
Kent City, Michigan 49330

whitedogenterprises.com

Published by WHITE DOG ENTERPRISES, Inc.
16060 Peach Ridge Avenue Kent City Michigan 49330

A subsidiary of The Paragon School of Pet Grooming, Inc.
110 Chicago Drive Jenison Michigan 49428

While the purpose of this book is for the enhanced grooming practices for professional pet
groomers and stylists, every effort has been made to showcase exceptional representation of all the
breeds, based on the written breed standard per the American Kennel Club, Inc. Many different
references and observations were chosen and combined to illustrate each dog individually and
perchance it may represent any one person's pet, property or work is purely coincidental.

ISBN Number: 978-0-692-88360-0

Printed in the United States

~ To My Mom ~
who instilled the love of animals deep into my heart.

Table of Contents

Introduction

Notes Pocket Pal was inspired by groomers across the country just like you. Hundreds of professionals have come to us raving about *Notes from the Grooming Table*. Although everyone loved the book as a reference guide, the one comment we heard over and over again was, "It is so big, I don't want to leave it out so it gets ruined!"

In response to your comments, we've created an abridged version of *Notes*. There are things you won't find in this easy-to-use mini guide. You won't find all the breeds with all their individual grooming directions, you won't find the step-by-step directions of how to wash or dry certain coat types—you are well beyond that in your professional career! What you **will** find in this handy little *Pocket Pal* are the nuts and bolts of how to properly execute a trim on a pet, while accentuating the breed profile—the backbone of all good grooming.

We pulled the parts you love best about *Notes from the Grooming Table*—the incredible art and directions strategically placed around the dog for easy reference—and put in into a little booklet that will easily slip into your smock pocket or grooming kit. This is not designed to be a replacement for *Notes from the Grooming Table*, however there are times that you just need a little reassurance to make sure you are doing the right thing for that breed.

Notes Pocket Pal is the simple little guide you need right at your fingertips to get the answers!

Happy Trimming!

Breed Facts & Characteristics

Country of Origin: *Central Europe*

Height at Shoulder: *9.5"–11½"*

Coat Length/Type: *Moderate/Wiry*

Color: *Black, black and tan, all shades of gray and red.*

Correct grooming procedure:
Hand-Strip

Common pet grooming practices:
Clipper-Trim

Correctly Groomed: Hand-Stripped
Typical blades used: #7F, #5F, #4F, short to medium guard combs, or a combination of those blades. Card coat after clipping to help maintain correct coat texture and color.

-The Goal-
Small, squarely built dog with a harsh, rough coat that is to be left about one inch in length on most of the dog with only minor neatening to accentuate its form.

Head is full and round: "monkey like."

Clear stop area to expose eyes.

Ears are clipped very close.

On mature dogs, neck coat will form a cape of longer hair.

Trim back side of tail and rear legs shorter to create a well-balanced, square outline.

Neaten muzzle area to create a well-balanced, round head style.

BLENDING AREA

Lightly clip sanitary areas: Under tail and tummy if needed with a #10.

Tidy leg coat to about 1" in length to form straight columns.

Neaten undercarriage line lightly.

Rear legs have moderate angulation.

Trim nails as short as possible or grind.

Shave pads and scissor feet round.

Neaten hocks.

General Description

This breed, done to breed standard, has a coat that is hand-stripped. For most Toy breeds, the primary emphasis is on the head. The body is compact, sturdy and squarely built. The pattern is based on basic bone and muscle structure. For pet dogs, whether hand-stripped or clipper-cut, the pattern is the same.

Ears are natural or cropped. In both cases, the fur on the entire ear is clipped very close, using a #10 or #15 blade on the outside of the leather and #40 on the inside. Edge ears with small detail finishing shears.

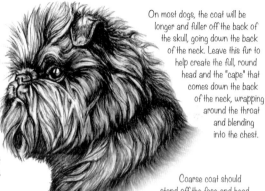

Clear the stop area with thinning shears or clippers to expose the round eye that looks straight forward.

On most dogs, the coat will be longer and fuller off the back of the skull, going down the back of the neck. Leave this fur to help create the full, round head and the "cape" that comes down the back of the neck, wrapping around the throat and blending into the chest.

Lightly shape the jaw line with thinning shears to create a neat but ragged appearance.

Coarse coat should stand off the face and head, serving as a frame to accentuate the round head and "monkey-like" expression, which is hallmark of this breed.

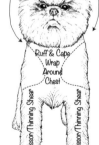

Ruff & Cape Wrap Around Chest

Scissor/Thinning Shear

Scissor/Thinning Shear

Round the head by hand-stripping or trimming with thinning shears. Expose ear tips. Clear stop area to show full, round eyes. Ruff wraps around neck to form a cape. Legs are trimmed about the same length as the body but shaped by hand to hide minor conformational faults. The tail is trimmed to the same length as body and can be either docked or undocked.

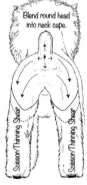

Blend round head into neck cape.

Scissor/Thinning Shear

Scissor/Thinning Shear

Airedale Terrier

Breed Facts & Characteristics

Country of Origin: *England*

Height at Shoulder: *22"–23"*

Coat Length/Type: *Hard/Wiry*

Color: *Black & Tan: black saddle, tan flatwork and furnishings.*

Correct grooming procedure:
Hand-Strip

Common pet grooming practices:
Clipper-Trim

> **-The Goal-**
> Everything about this breed is tight and tailored. The well-toned body is accentuated by the groom. Head is rectangular in shape. All pattern lines are invisible.

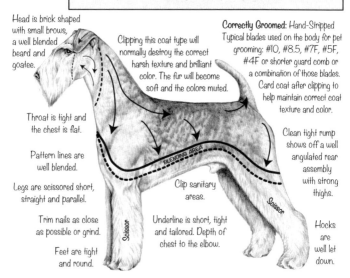

Head is brick shaped with small brows, a well blended beard and goatee.

Clipping this coat type will normally destroy the correct harsh texture and brilliant color. The fur will become soft and the colors muted.

Correctly Groomed: Hand-Stripped Typical blades used on the body for pet grooming: #10, #8.5, #7F, #5F, #4F or shorter guard comb or a combination of those blades. Card coat after clipping to help maintain correct coat texture and color.

Throat is tight and the chest is flat.

Pattern lines are well blended.

Legs are scissored short, straight and parallel.

Trim nails as close as possible or grind.

Feet are tight and round.

BLENDING AREA

Clip sanitary areas.

Underline is short, tight and tailored. Depth of chest to the elbow.

Scissor

Clean tight rump shows off a well angulated rear assembly with strong thighs.

Hocks are well let down.

Scissor

General Description

Everything about the Airedale is tight and tailored. This is a dog of great strength, power and agility. They are known as the "King of Terriers." When grooming an Airedale, remember there is nothing soft or fluffy about the breed. In the finished groom, there is very little coat hiding the contours of its body. The leg coat is slightly longer. The head is rectangular in shape with a piercing expression, moderate muzzle coat and small brows.

Their expression is friendly but alert and courageous. Head is brick shaped with small brows and a well blended beard and goatee. The top skull and the muzzle are equal in length with the stop area being the center point. All lines on the head are invisible.

Clip top skull with blades ranging from a #7F to a #5F, with the grain.

The eyebrows are very small, split at the stop area. There are no sharp lines. Shape and blend with thinning shears.

On the muzzle, the hair is longer but not so long as to extend beyond the planes of the top skull or cheeks. Blend the bulk of the muzzle with thinning shears or skim with a medium guard comb. Lightly trim the end of the muzzle to accentuate the rectangular head style. The lines at the side of the face are well blended and straight. Do not hollow out under the eye.

Use a #10 or #15 blade on the outside of the ear, a #40 blade can be used on the inside of the ear leather with a very light touch. Edge the ear with small detailing shears. The fold of the ear comes to just above the line of the top skull.

Blend Well
Blend Well
Blend Well
Transitional Blending Area
Blend Well

The throat is trimmed close with a #7F used against the grain or a #10 or #15 blade used with the coat growth.

Ear Safety Tip:
Remember, always keep the tips of the shears towards the tips of the ears when edging for safety.

Stay inside the natural cowlick line of the neck that runs from the ear bulb down in a "U" or "V" shape. Stop about 3 or 4 finger widths above the breast bone. Thinning shear the cowlick seam to blend with the longer coat of the neck.

From the front and rear, the legs drop in straight, parallel lines from well-toned shoulders and thighs. When setting the pattern, use the turn of the muscles to set the lines. Chest is flat but use caution not to bald out this area due to cowlicks where the front legs join the chest. Rear is short, tight and clean. Leg furnishings are slightly longer than the body coat.

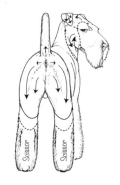

Scissor Scissor Scissor

Scissor Scissor

Breed Facts & Characteristics

Country of Origin: *Australia*

Height at Shoulder: *10"–11"*

Coat Length/Type: *Hard/Wiry*

Color: *Blue and tan, sandy, or red; topknot is silver or a shade lighter than head color.*

Correct grooming procedure:
Brush Out/Hand-Strip

Common pet grooming practices:
Clipper-Trim/Hand-Strip

-The Goal-
This breed is small and spunky. The body coat should range from 1–2 inches, longer over back of the neck. The coat is harsh and shiny. Ears and feet are free of long hair.

Ears clipped clean.

Head has longer coat on the top of the head, blending into a ruff on the neck. Muzzle fur is shorter and tight.

Thinning Shear

Ruff wraps around neck and shoulders into chest and throat area.

Correctly Groomed: Hand-Stripped
A combination of longer blades or short to medium guard combs are the typical blades used on the body for pet grooming.

Tail is short.

Rump blends down into longer furnishings on the rear legs. No excessive coat hanging off rear end.

Pattern lines are invisible.

BLENDING AREA

Legs are lightly coated. Lower leg and foot are free of long hair. Feathering off rear of front leg only.

Thinning Shear

Tidy undercarriage line.

Thinning Shear

Hocks are free of long hair.

Thinning shear or clip lower legs with blade a #10 or #7F blade.

Trim nails as close as possible or grind.

General Description

The Australian Terrier is a small, hearty working terrier. He is rectangular in outline with a level topline and a docked tail. Chest is deep, reaching to just below elbows with a well-developed keel. Has a harsh, straight outer jacket with a distinctive ruff wrapping around neck and shoulders. The coat is about 2½ inches long but much shorter on lower legs and feet. Furnishings on top of head are softer and finer in texture. Has upright triangular ears which are free of long hair. Keen expression complements bright, alert and self-confident nature.

Head is covered with harsh coat, longer on the top of the skull, shorter on the muzzle and cheeks. Hand-strip or trim the muzzle and the cheeks leaving about ½–1" of coat. Cheeks should be flat with a small dark spot exposed just behind the eye on the zygomatic arch. The shorter coat on muzzle and cheeks will stop about a finger's width before the ear opening, framing in the face. On the lower jaw, the coat is shorter, transitioning into the throat and ruff right at the neck and throat junction. On top of head, coat is about 2" in length and slightly messy in appearance. The ruff will be longer blending into the chest area.

Entire ear short—strip longer hair or use a #15 on the outside of the leather and a closer blade in the inside.

Top skull is covered with harsh coat about 2 inches long and should look messy and wild.

Clear stop area with thinners or by hand-stripping.

Coat naturally shorter on top of muzzle.

Coat on muzzle between ½ to 1 inch long.

Sides of cheeks are flat and short.

On the lower jaw, the coat is shorter, transitioning into the throat and ruff right at the neck and throat junction.

Edge ears with shears.

Leave a finger's width of longer hair ahead of the ear canal.

Dark spot of shorter coat right behind eye.

Fur coming off the back and sides of neck is longer, blending into the throat and chest.

Clean Ear Tips

Head is covered with harsh, somewhat longer fur than the body. Muzzle has shorter coat forming a wedge shape. There are two shorter spots of coat just behind the eyes. Coat on neck is longer, wrapping around the neck forming a cape into the chest area. The cape blends invisibly to the shorter body coat. From the front and rear, the legs drop in straight, parallel lines from well-toned shoulders and thighs. Feet are very tight and short. Under the tail is short and clean with a drape of longer fur covering the back of the thighs. Leg furnishings are hard and wiry, slightly longer than the body coat.

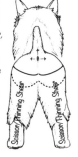

Breed Facts & Characteristics

Country of Origin: *England*

Height at Shoulder: *15"–17½"*

Coat Length/Type: *Curly/Thick*

Color: *Blue, sandy, liver, blue and tan, liver and tan.*

Correct grooming procedure:
Hand-Scissor

Common pet grooming practices:
Clipper-Trim

> -The Goal-
> Everything about this breed is curved and graceful. Their curly coat
> and unique head style makes them look similar to a small lamb.

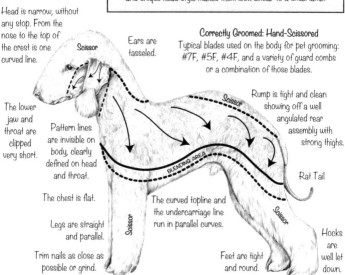

Head is narrow, without any stop. From the nose to the top of the crest is one curved line.

Scissor

Ears are tasseled.

The lower jaw and throat are clipped very short.

Pattern lines are invisible on body, clearly defined on head and throat.

The chest is flat.

Legs are straight and parallel.

Trim nails as close as possible or grind.

Correctly Groomed: Hand-Scissored
Typical blades used on the body for pet grooming: #7F, #5F, #4F, and a variety of guard combs or a combination of those blades.

Scissor

Rump is tight and clean showing off a well angulated rear assembly with strong thighs.

BLENDING AREA

Rat Tail

The curved topline and the undercarriage line run in parallel curves.

Scissor

Scissor

Feet are tight and round.

Hocks are well let down.

General Description

The Bedlington is unique to the terrier group with its narrow, well-balanced, flexible and flowing body outline. It has a silhouette more like a sighthound than most terriers. The coat consists of harsh guard hair combined with a soft, dense undercoat. The traditional Bedlington trim is highly stylized, with a distinctive head style, tasseled ears and a rat tail. This is a graceful little dog with true terrier spunk.

Head Study — Bedlington Terrier

The head is unique with its lamb-like appearance. The skull is narrow, long and graceful. The eyes peek out from the sides of the head. The lower jaw is clipped clean and the ears are neatly tasseled. All lines on the head are clean and sharp.

The highest point of the topknot will be above the occiput and in a direct line from the front edge of the ear. This high point of the head will blend down into the scissored neck.

The eyes will be exposed from the side of the head only. The entire stop area is filled in with fur to create the lamb look of the head.

On the narrow head, the fur creates a soft arch from the nose to the peak of the occiput. Comb all the fur over to one side of the skull and cut off any hair that falls outside the planes of the skull. Trim one side all the way from the nose to above the ear, then repeat on the opposite side. Once the excessive hair is removed from the sides, trim the top line in a light, curving arch when viewed from profile.

The throat and cheeks and lower jaw are trimmed close with a #10 or #15 blade used against the grain.

Use a #10 or #15 blade on the outside of the ear. A #40 blade can be used on the inside of the ear leather with a very light touch. The tassel covers the bottom ⅓ to ¼ of the ear tip. Edge the ear with small detailing shears. The ear is low set, roughly in line with the eye.

Ear Safety Tip:
Remember, always keep the tips of the shears towards the tips of the ears when edging for safety.

Stay inside the natural cowlick line of the neck that runs from the ear bulb down in a "U" or "V" shape. Stop about 2 or 3 finger widths above the breast bone. The line is very sharp and clean.

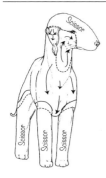

The head is unique, looking like a lamb with tasseled ears. The body is very narrow. The front and rear legs drop in parallel lines, toeing in a little bit on the front feet creating a "keyhole" front. Coat on the legs is only long enough to create the parallel lines from the body. Feet are very tight. Tail is shaved at the end to form the characteristic "rat tail."

Breed Facts & Characteristics

Country of Origin: *Mediterranean*

Height at Shoulder: *9½"–11½"*

Coat Length/Type: *Curly/Thick*

Color: *All white but some cream or biscuit coloring is allowed.*

Correct grooming procedure:
Scissor-Trim

Common pet grooming practices:
Clipper-Trim or Scissor-Trim

-The Goal-
The fur should look like a powderpuff, void of any marks or lines. The coat needs to be totally mat free. The outline should be velvet smooth and neat. The breed is to be well-balanced, slightly longer than tall.

Hand-scissor top of head.

Head is broad and rounded with deep set eyes.

Scissor

The ears reach to the nose. This proportion sets up the entire balance for the rest of the round head style. Jawline is level with ears.

Either hand-scissor entire dog or use a guard comb to set the basic pattern. Pet dogs can be modified into shorter trim styles using the same basic pattern.

Tail is left long and natural.

Show off a powerful rear by accentuating a well angulated hind-end. Use the thigh muscle to set the pattern line.

Blend

Neck is long, arched and powerful. Leave coat a bit longer than that on the body.

Hand-scissor or clip main body section

Blend

Lowest point of pattern should be at bend.

Legs fall in parallel lines from the shoulder. Use the shoulder muscle to set pattern line.

Blend

Scissor

Deep through chest.

Slight rise into the tuck-up area.

Scissor

Hocks are well let down.

Feet are rounded and face straight forward.

Pads are trimmed close.

General Description

The Bichon Frise is an active, happy little dog with great enthusiasm for life. Everything about the look of this breed is soft and rounded, thus earning it the label of "powderpuff." Their bodies are compact, yet they are longer than they are tall. The fun loving, curious expression is set off by deep dark eyes and a dark nose. The coat is curly and dense and considered non-shedding. Their color is always white, but a small amount of cream or biscuit is allowed.

Head Study   Bichon Frise

Shape the top of the head into an smooth, even extension of the skull. The coat is softly rounded with curved shears to create a well formed head style that balances with the overall trim and blends into the neck. There are no breaks over the ears.

Bevel topknot line steeply so it's very short right above eyes, getting longer as it moves out and away from eyes. Bevel area doesn't exceed much beyond outside corners of the eyes.

Once the ear length is trimmed to the end of the nose, the amount of fur left on the jaw will be determined. The ears and jawline should be equal. Round the jawline with large, curved shears. The coat at the end of the muzzle will be beveled to blend with the longer coat of the jaw.

The throat is clipped with the same blade used on the body or it can be slightly shorter.

Their expression is friendly and alert. The topknot, ears and muzzle all lend themselves to a balanced, well rounded head style with no broken lines. The dark eyes and nose are at the center of the head. The eyes are deep set. The ear feathering is equal in length to the nose.

The only way to get the correct look and size for the Bichon head style is to leave the neck fuller, blending the rounded topknot into the crested neck. The fuller neck will extend to the withers area based on the conformation of the pet and the length of the trim. The longer the trim, the farther the neck line will extend. The fuller coat on the neck should look very natural, enhancing a long neck and upright head style.

Softly round the ends of the ears to the length of the nose. The top of the ear should blend seamlessly into the topknot without any lines or indentations.

The eyes and nose are at the center of the round head piece. Ears are level with the jaw line. At transition points between the body and the legs, blend the lines so they are invisible. The legs should fall into straight columns, from the body to the rounded feet, when viewed from the front or rear. There are no breaks in the pattern anywhere on the dog.

Breed Facts & Characteristics

Country of Origin: *Russia*

Height at Shoulder: *26"–30"*

Coat Length/Type: *Longer/Wavy*

Color: *Black*

Correct grooming procedure:
Card/Clip/Scissor

Common pet grooming practices:
Card/Clip/Scissor

Trim a square right at the center of the skull to start the rectangular shape of the head with a #10 or #7 blade.

Clip ears short.

Full fall over eyes.

Head is massive with a rectangular shape. Trim just enough coat from the cheek and jaw area to accentuate the look.

Throat is clipped very short to just above the breast bone.

Chest is prominent.

-The Goal-
Breed is large, powerful, and slightly longer than tall. The "tousled" double coat should be a combination of harsh and soft textures. Coat should be clean and mat free. Head is full and rectangular with a heavy fall over the eyes.

Card out the undercoat on the body. Clipper-cut the bulk of the body with a longer guard comb so there is about 1–2 inches of coat left on the body.

BLENDING AREA

Clip sanitary areas.

Rump is tight and clean showing off a well-angulated rear assembly with strong thighs.

Scissor rear legs full to match front.

Scissor legs in full, straight columns from shoulder.

Trim nails as short as possible or grind.

Shave pads and round feet.

General Description

The Black Russian Terrier is very powerful with great courage and endurance. Everything about this breed is immense. Their outline is almost square with a massive head that is in proportion to the size of the body and approximately the same length as the neck. The chest reaches to the elbows. Withers are high yet the back is level. The tail may be natural or docked. The coat is "tousled" with a combination of harsh guard coat and soft undercoat. It is trimmed and styled to 1–4 inches in length over much of the body and legs. The head is blocky with flat top skull and an untrimmed veil of hair covering the eyes and muzzle. The ears are natural and triangular in shape.

Head Study

The fall is created by leaving all the coat covering the eyes. Use the eye socket ridge as your guide for the start of the fall. This will create a full fall of hair over the eyes and stop area. Do *not* split the brows nor trim the outer edges of the fall near the eyes.

The head is well-balanced to the body of the dog and should give the impression or power and strength.

Leave fall natural.

Clip ears very close with a #10 or #15 on the outside and as close as a #40 on the inside, used with a very light touch. Edge ears with small detailing shears to finish.

The beard and mustache are left full and natural to highlight the impressive scale of the head piece.

Trim the jowl area on and angle to accentuate a rectangular head.

The throat is clipped very close with a #10 or #15 in reverse. Start just under the ear bulb, trimming in a "U" shape to 2 to 3 fingers above the breast bone.

Slightly longer coat is left on the back of the neck to create a "mane" down to the withers.

The top of the skull is flat. Accentuate this by clipping a square shape just behind the eyes with a #7F or a #5F, creating "platform." Blend the short coat into the longer coat on the top of the head at the outer edges of the box so the lines are invisible but leave the fall area long and natural.

On the head, the fall is full and natural without any trimming. The throat line is crisp and clean. At transition points on the body, blend the lines so they are invisible. Legs should be left fuller and fall into straight columns, from the body to the feet, on both the front and rear legs. The chest is full, rounded in shape.

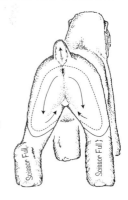

Scissor Full

Bouvier des Flandres

Breed Facts & Characteristics

Country of Origin: *France*

Height at Shoulder: *23½"–27½"*

Coat Length/Type: *Harsh/Long*

Color: *Black, gray or fawn. Typical to see salt and pepper or brindled markings in the coat.*

Correct grooming procedure:
Hand-Strip

Common pet grooming practices:
Clipper-Trim

> **-The Goal-**
> This breed is a rugged, powerfully built square-bodied dog. The coat should feel harsh to the touch, yet clean and mat free. Head is full and round with a fall over the eyes. Body coat is approximately 2–2½" long.

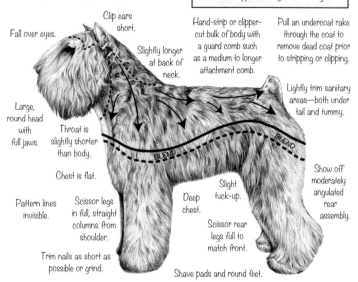

Top of head with #5F, #4F or medium guard comb against the grain.

Clip ears short.

Fall over eyes.

Slightly longer at back of neck.

Hand-strip or clipper-cut bulk of body with a guard comb such as a medium to longer attachment comb.

Pull an undercoat rake through the coat to remove dead coat prior to stripping or clipping.

Lightly trim sanitary areas—both under tail and tummy.

Large, round head with full jaws.

Throat is slightly shorter than body.

BLEND

BLEND

Chest is flat.

Show off moderately angulated rear assembly.

Pattern lines invisible.

Scissor legs in full, straight columns from shoulder.

Deep chest.

Slight tuck-up.

Scissor rear legs full to match front.

Trim nails as short as possible or grind.

Shave pads and round feet.

General Description

The Bouvier des Flandres is an all-purpose farm dog. The dog should look square in outline, very powerful and robust with a rough coat, massive head and strong neck. This dog has great strength but should not look heavy or coarse.

Head Study

Bouvier des Flandres

The flat top skull is accentuated by clipping it close with a #5F, or #4F with the grain, or a longer guard comb against the grain.

Ears can be cropped or natural. Clip very close with a #10 or #15 on the outside and as close as a #40 on the inside, used with a very light touch. Edge ears with small detailing shears to finish.

Fall is created by following the eye socket ridge. Leave all hair between the eyes in the stop area. Eyes are exposed by scissoring in an arch over the eye. Fur is very short at the back corner of the eye, and gets longer towards the nose. Do *not* split the brows.

The neck is arched. If a dog does not have this naturally, leave the coat on the back of the neck a bit fuller to create it.

The beard and mustache are left full and natural to highlight the impressive scale of the head piece

The jowls are left full. The line that separates the head from the neck starts at the ear bulb and follows in a semi-circle, under the throat and back up to the opposite ear bulb.

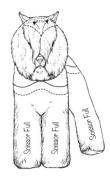

At transition points on the body, blend the lines so they are invisible.

Legs should be left fuller and fall into straight columns, from the body to the feet, on both the front and rear legs. The chest should be flat, but use caution not to bald out this area due to cowlicks found where the front legs meet the chest.

Scissor Full
Scissor Full
Scissor Full

Scissor Full
Scissor Full

Breed Facts & Characteristics

Country of Origin: *Belgium*

Height at Shoulder: *7"–9"*

Coat Length/Type: *Moderate/Wiry*

Color: *Reds, black and tan, black, or a combination of red and black hairs over the body with a black mask on the face. Lighter colored dogs may have a dark mask.*

Correct grooming procedure:
Hand-Strip

Common pet grooming practices:
Clipper-Trim

-The Goal-
Rough coated variety has a neat body outline. The facial expression is almost "human-like." Body coat should be short, hard and very close fitting to the body. Hand-stripping is the only way to retain this proper coat texture.

Hand-strip top of skull and cheek area very tightly to show off a large, round head with naturally domed forehead.

Clear stop area to expose eyes.

Ears clipped very close.

If hand-stripping, card body first to remove bulk of loose undercoat. Follow by hand-stripping hard outer coat. As new hair grows in, it will be harsh and tight fitting to the body. Always pull in direction of the coat growth. Legs, too.

Trim back side of tail and rear legs shorter to create a well-balanced, neat, square outline.

The muzzle, jaw and above the eyes can have slightly longer coat to accentuate the "human expression." Lower jaw is undershot.

Lightly clip sanitary areas: Under tail and tummy if needed with a #10.

Tidy leg coat to about 1" in length to form straight columns.

Lightly neaten undercarriage line.

BLENDING AREA

Rear legs have moderate angulation.

Trim nails as short as possible or grind.

If clipping, typical blades used on the body for pet grooming: #7F, #5F, #4F, short to medium guard combs, or a combination of those blades. Card coat after clipping to help maintain correct coat texture and color.

Neaten hocks.

Shave pads and scissor feet round.

General Description

This breed, done to breed standard, has a coat that is hand-stripped. For most Toy breeds, the primary emphasis is on the head. The body is compact, sturdy and squarely built. The pattern is based on basic bone and muscle structure. For pet dogs, whether hand-stripped or clipper-cut, the pattern is the same.

Ears are natural or cropped. In both cases, the fur on the entire ear is clipped very close, using a #10 or #15 blade on the outside of the leather and #40 on the inside. Edge ears with small detail finishing shears keeping the tips of the shears towards the tips of the ears.

The top skull is covered with short coat conforming to the natural roundness of the skull. Use a #7F, #5F, or a 4F on the top skull or hand-strip the top of the head close. Due to the deep stop, rounded skull and forward facing eyes, only a tiny bit of added coat is needed to form the eyebrows. Use the eye socket rim to create the brows.

Clear the stop area with thinning shears or clippers to expose the large, round eyes that look straight forward.

The coat on the jaw is left longer. Lightly shape the jaw line with thinning shears into a curved shape. The jaw on this breed must be undershot.

The cheeks and throat are smooth and clean. Blades ranging from a #10 to a #15, used with or against the grain, are common in pet styling.

The natural cowlick line assists with setting the throat area. Create a soft "V" or "U" shape coming about 2 finger widths above the breast bone.

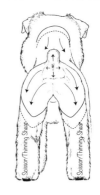

The top of the round head is trimmed close, showing off a deep stop and domed skull. Ears are trimmed very close. Clear stop area to show full, round eyes. The lower jaw is undershot. Shape the entire lower jaw into a rounded fashion to show off this unique trait for this breed. Legs are trimmed about the same length as the body but shaped by hand to hide minor conformational faults. The tail is trimmed to the same length as body.

Breed Facts & Characteristics

Country of Origin: *Scotland*

Height at Shoulder: *9½"–10"*

Coat Length/Type: *Hard/Wiry*

Color: *Any color except white.*

Correct grooming procedure:

Card & Hand-Strip

Common pet grooming practices:

Clipper-Trim/Hand-Strip

Correctly Groomed: Hand-Strip

Typical blades used on the body for pet grooming: #7F, #5F, #4F, short to medium guard combs, or a combination of those blades. Card coat after clipping to help maintain correct coat texture and color.

-The Goal-
This is a small, tough terrier. They have a harsh outer coat and a thick undercoat. They have a round head style with a keen, foxy expression. Pattern lines on the body are invisible.

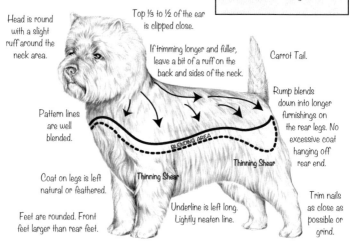

Head is round with a slight ruff around the neck area.

Top ⅓ to ½ of the ear is clipped close.

If trimming longer and fuller, leave a bit of a ruff on the back and sides of the neck.

Carrot Tail.

Rump blends down into longer furnishings on the rear legs. No excessive coat hanging off rear end.

Pattern lines are well blended.

BLENDING AREA

Thinning Shear

Coat on legs is left natural or feathered.

Thinning Shear

Feet are rounded. Front feet larger than rear feet.

Underline is left long. Lightly neaten line.

Trim nails as close as possible or grind.

General Description

This is a small, spunky terrier designed to go to ground after all types of vermin. The body is covered with a harsh, moderate length coat. The head is round in shape with small, erect ears. The tail is well covered with hard hair but never feathered. The Cairn Terrier should look neat but "un-groomed."

Head Study
Cairn Terrier

Their expression is friendly, bold and full of life. Head is full and round. The ears are small, triangular and erect. The eyes are deep set. When viewed from the front, the eyes and nose are at the center of the circle. When finished, the head is well blended and very natural looking.

Comb the fur forward, over the brows. With thinning shears, trim a frame around the eye area. The line is beveled with a deep set eye.

Pull the hair up, trimming the coat on the top of the head, to just below the ear tips using thinning shears.

Trim the stop area lightly with thinning shears before framing the eye area.

The lower line of the head completes the circle that puts the eyes and nose at the center of the head piece when looking at the pet from the front. The lower line parallels the jaw bone. Comb all the coat down and trim with shears in a curved line running from the nose all the way up to behind the occiput. Soften the line with thinning shears to complete the head piece.

The top ⅓ to ½ of the ear tip is clipped. Use a # 10 or #15 blade on the outside of the ear, a #40 blade can be used on the inside of the ear leather with a very light touch. Edge the ear with small detailing shears.

Ear Safety Tip:
Remember, always keep the tips of the shears towards the tips of the ears when edging for safety.

The line at the back of the skull is about an inch beyond the occiput, if trimming with clippers. If hand-stripping, there is a ruff of harsh coat that wraps around the neck.

The throat is slightly shorter than the body.

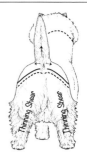

The head is round and full with eyes and nose at the center. From the front and rear, the legs drop straight, parallel lines from well-toned shoulder and thighs. When setting in the pattern, use the turn of the muscles to set the lines. Under the tail is short and clean with a drape of longer fur covering the back of the thighs. Leg furnishings are slightly longer than the body coat. Tail is a carrot shaped and very short on the back side.

Breed Facts & Characteristics

Country of Origin: *Czechoslovakia*

Height at Shoulder: *10"-13"*

Coat Length/Type: *Long/Silky*

Color: *Shades of gray from charcoal to platinum.*

Correct grooming procedure:
Clipper-Trim

Common pet grooming practices:
Clipper-Trim

Correctly Groomed: Clipper-Cut

Pattern lines are unique. Blades used on the body for pet grooming are a #5F or #4F on the bulk of the back and body. In the throat, shoulder and rump areas, a #10 or #15 blade is used to keep the neck tight while clearly exposing the muscles of the shoulder and hip areas.

-The Goal-
The haircut should show off a strong, lean and well muscled terrier type dog. Pattern lines on the body are distinct, flowing smoothly into the longer feathering.

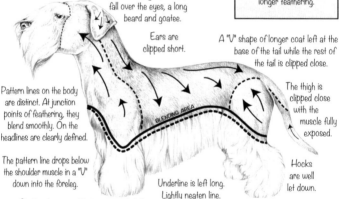

Head is rectangular with a fall over the eyes, a long beard and goatee.

Ears are clipped short.

A "V" shape of longer coat left at the base of the tail while the rest of the tail is clipped close.

Pattern lines on the body are distinct. At junction points of feathering, they blend smoothly. On the headlines are clearly defined.

The thigh is clipped close with the muscle fully exposed.

BLENDING AREA

The pattern line drops below the shoulder muscle in a "V" down into the foreleg.

Underline is left long. Lightly neaten line.

Hocks are well let down.

Coat on legs is left natural.

Feet are rounded. Front feet larger than rear feet.

Trim nails as close as possible or grind.

General Description

The Cesky is short legged terrier, one and a half times longer than it is tall and has a topline that rises slightly over the loin and rump. The head is twice as long as it is wide. Everything about this breed shows off a powerful, muscular body yet the breed is lean and graceful. The clipped coat is soft and the furnishings are long and silky. The Cesky is trimmed to emphasize a slim but powerful body type. The head is well furnished with a classic terrier rectangular outline, triangular ears and a fall over the eyes. The tail is long and slender.

Their expression is alert and bold. Head is rectangular with a long fall of hair over the stop area with a full beard and goatee. The topskull and the muzzle are equal in length with the stop area being the center point. All lines on the head are clean and sharp.

The line for the fall follows the eye socket rim. The back corners of the eyes are trimmed closely to expose the eye. This line arches out towards the nose. It is crisp and clean.

On the muzzle, the hair is long and natural but does not break the line of the topskull. When combing down the beard, the lines at the side of the face form a straight plane.

Just below the back corner of the eyes, the fur is short and well blended, creating fill under the eye. The clipper lines of the beard are clean and sharp.

The throat is trimmed close with a #10 or #15 used against the grain.

Clip topskull with blades ranging from a #7F to a #5F, used against the grain or blades ranging from a #10 to #15 with the grain.

Use a #10 or #15 blade on the outside of the ear, a #40 blade can be used on the inside of the ear leather with a very light touch. Edge the ear with small detailing shears. The fold of the ear is level with the line of the topskull.

Ear Safety Tip: Remember, always keep the tips of the shears towards the tips of the ears when edging for safety.

Stay inside the natural cowlick line of the neck that runs from the ear bulb down in a "U" or "V" shape. Stop about 2 or 3 finger widths above the breast bone. Thinning shear the cowlick seam to blend with the longer coat of the neck.

Leave Long

Clean & Sharp

Transitional Blending Area

The head is long and rectangular with a fall of hair between the eyes. From the front and rear, the legs drop straight from muscular shoulders and thighs. When setting the pattern, use the turn of the muscles to set the lines. Under the tail is short and clean with a drape of longer fur covering the back of the thighs. Leg furnishings are longer than the body.

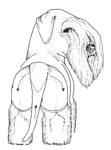

Breed Facts & Characteristics

Country of Origin: *England*

Height at Shoulder: *14"–15"*

Coat Length/Type: *Soft/Thick*

Color: *Wide variety of colors. Reds, creams, browns, black, black and tan, parti colored with white, and tricolored. For multi-colored dogs, the color should be clear and crisp with roaning and flecking allowable on dogs with white making up their base color patterns.*

The head is domed with a crown of fur above the eyes. The back section of the skull is clipped close. Thinning shear the line of the crown where it meets the back skull.

Use a damp towel to go over the muzzle after the bath.

Clip muzzle if needed.

Clip top ⅓ of ear leather, or to jawline.

The throat is trimmed close with a #10 or #15.

The coat should look as natural as possible and all transitional pattern lines should be invisible.

Trim nails as close as possible or grind.

Shave pads.

BLENDING AREA

Neaten undercarriage line into a soft arch. Highest point of arch is directly below last rib.

Bevel feet into circles; bevel line on front legs blends smoothly into rear feet as one flowing line, if coat is full enough.

Correct grooming procedure:
Card & Hand-Strip

Common pet grooming practices:
Clipper-Trim

-The Goal-
The coat should be fresh smelling, light and shiny. The natural body jacket should lay tight to the body. If clipping, no clipper marks. The long feathering floats as the dog moves. All long fur is totally mat free.

Correctly Groomed: Hand-Strip
Typical blades used on the body for pet grooming; #10, #9, #8.5, #7F, #5F or #4F or a combination of those blades.

Remove long coat from underside of the tail.

Thin the thigh area slightly to accentuate the muscle.

Round and bevel the hocks.

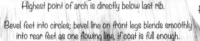

General Description

The American Cocker Spaniel is the smallest of the gun dogs. It is well-balanced, compact and firmly built with great speed and endurance. The chest is deep, reaching to the elbows. The topline is level or slightly sloping. The docked tail is an extension of the topline. The head is well-balanced with a rounded skull, pronounced stop and full lips. The ears are long and the expression soft, kind and intelligent. The coat is soft and silky, and found in a number of color combinations. The coat should lie smoothly over the head, throat, neck, shoulders, back, down the sides of the dog and the thighs. There is much longer and profuse feathering on the ears, chest, undercarriage, belly and legs.

Head Study · Cocker Spaniel

The Cocker has a rounded skull, a deep stop and a soft, kind expression. To accentuate these traits, there is a crown of fur above the eyes to about half way back on the skull. The back section of the skull is clipped close with a #10 or #15 with the grain or a #7F in reverse, following the ridge where the head and neck meet. With thinning shears blend the line of the crown and the short fur of the back skull. The line is well blended when done and the crown looks very natural.

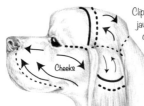

The end of the muzzle and lips are clipped with a #10 or #15 blade. If the dog is very light coated, do not trim muzzle area.

Cheeks

Clip top ⅓ of ear leather or to the jawline with a #10 or #15 blade, creating a soft dip at the blending line. Neaten the clipped edge of the front of the ear with small shears. Neaten bottom of ear feathering so it's rounded and neat.

The throat is trimmed close with a #7F, #10 or #15, with or against the grain. This area can also be left natural on light coated pets.

Throat

Ear Safety Tip:
Always keep the tips of the shears towards the tips of the ears when edging for safety.

Stay inside the natural cowlick line of the neck that runs from the ear bulb down in a "U" or"V" shape. Stop about 3 or 4 finger widths above the breast bone. Thinning shear the cowlick seam to blend with the longer coat of the neck.

The Cocker has higher pattern lines than many breeds. The blending areas start midway up on the shoulder. Actual placement of the pattern lines can vary based on client preference and how much coat the dog has naturally. Furnishings are left long and natural. Bevels are neatly flared. The line of the bevel can vary but they should be even on all four feet.

Modified Show Trim In General

This trim mimics the full show trim style in an easier-to-care-for version. Some owners go a step further and have a large section of the underbelly clipped short as well. This allows the longer furnishings to drape over and conceal the clipped section while the pet is standing.

> **-The Goal-**
> The coat should be fresh smelling, light and shiny. Clipper and scissor work is smooth and even. All longer fur is totally mat free.

The coat should look as natural as possible and all transitional pattern lines should be invisible.

Correctly Groomed: Hand-Strip
Typical blades used on the body for pet grooming; #10, #9, #8.5, #7F, #5F or #4F or a combination of those blades.

On furnishings, hand-scissor the coat to a consistent length between 2–4 inches. Keep the tips of the shears pointed towards the table top to minimize scissor marks. Blend with thinning shears to finish.

BLENDING AREA

Bulk thin the thigh area slightly to accentuate the muscle.

Bevel feet into circles. Box the foot in first, then round neatly with shears. Double check work multiple times.

Shave pads.

Legs are hand-scissored very full. They fall in straight columns or can flair slightly out to large neatly beveled feet. Bulk thin at the pattern line so it blends seamlessly into the longer furnishings.

Pet Trim In General

This trim is a low maintenance version that captures the essence of the breed. On the furnishings for very active pets whose coats easily form mats, opt for the shorter blades ranging from the #4F blade to shorter to medium guard comb to create the trim. For owners willing to brush between grooming appointments, longer guard combs work well for this trim style.

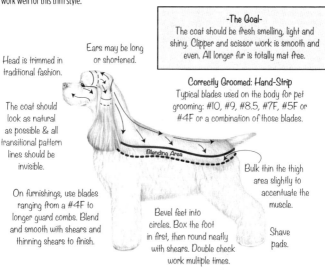

-The Goal-
The coat should be fresh smelling, light and shiny. Clipper and scissor work is smooth and even. All longer fur is totally mat free.

Head is trimmed in traditional fashion.

Ears may be long or shortened.

Correctly Groomed: Hand-Strip
Typical blades used on the body for pet grooming: #10, #9, #8.5, #7F, #5F or #4F or a combination of those blades.

The coat should look as natural as possible & all transitional pattern lines should be invisible.

Blending Area

Bulk thin the thigh area slightly to accentuate the muscle.

On furnishings, use blades ranging from a #4F to longer guard combs. Blend and smooth with shears and thinning shears to finish.

Bevel feet into circles. Box the foot in first, then round neatly with shears. Double check work multiple times.

Shave pads.

The Cocker has higher pattern lines than many breeds. The blending areas start midway up on the shoulder. Actual placement of the pattern lines can vary based on client preference and how much coat the dog has naturally. Legs fall in straight columns to neatly beveled feet.

Dachshund (Wire Haired)

Breed Facts & Characteristics

Country of Origin: *Europe*

Height at Shoulder: *7"–11"*

Coat Length/Type: *Combination/Wiry*

Color: *Common colors are red or black and tan. Other colors are acceptable including: brown, fawn, gray, all with tan points; a mixture of black, brown and gray hair known as wild boar; all shades of red or blue dapples, as well as brindled.*

Correct grooming procedure:
Hand-Strip

Common pet grooming practices:
Clipper-Trim or Hand-Strip

> **-The Goal-**
> From a distance, this variety should resemble its smooth hair cousin with the exception of the distinctive brows and beard. The body coat, including the tail, should be short, hard and very close fitting to the body. Hand-stripping is the only way to retain this proper coat texture.

Top of the skull should be hand-stripped very short. Leave two tufts of fur over the eyes to form the divided, triangular eyebrows. Shape brows with shears.

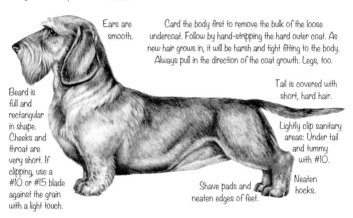

Ears are smooth.

Card the body first to remove the bulk of the loose undercoat. Follow by hand-stripping the hard outer coat. As new hair grows in, it will be harsh and tight fitting to the body. Always pull in the direction of the coat growth. Legs, too.

Beard is full and rectangular in shape. Cheeks and throat are very short. If clipping, use a #10 or #15 blade against the grain with a light touch.

Tail is covered with short, hard hair.

Lightly clip sanitary areas: Under tail and tummy with #10.

Shave pads and neaten edges of feet.

Neaten hocks.

General Description
Except for its head, the wire-coated Dachshund would almost look like the smooth variety. On the head, the eyes are framed by eyebrows and the muzzle is covered with a rectangular beard. The ears are almost smooth and void of any long hair. The body, tail and legs are covered with a thick, tight-fitting jacket of harsh coat.

Head Study — Dachshund (Wire Haired)

Shape the arched eyebrows by following the eye socket ridge. Brows are split at the stop area. Use curved shears in reverse to help set the brow. The coat is very short at the back of the eye and gets longer towards the nose.

Or clipper the top skull very close. If clipping, use blades ranging from a #10 used with the grain a #4F used against the grain depending on the coat density.

The occiput is the dividing line between the head and the neck.

The ears should be smooth and fine. Remove long hair by hand-stripping or clipping with blades ranging from a #10 or #15 on the outside and a #40 on the inside. Finish by edging the ears with small detailing shears.

The beard and mustache form a rectangular head style. When viewed from straight on, the cheeks and the beard should form one continuous line.

The cheeks and throat are smooth and clean. Blades ranging from a #10 to a #15, used with or against the grain, are common in pet styling. The line runs from the back corner of the eye to the cheek whisker nodule, to the chin nodule, up to the opposite cheek whisker nodule and opposite eye. Use the zygomatic arch to set the line from the back corner of the eye to the ear canal. The natural cowlick line assists with setting the throat area. Create a soft "V" or "U" shape coming about 2 finger widths above the breast bone.

The Wire Haired Dachshund does not have a distinct pattern. They look very "natural" when finished. The coat should be carded and hand-stripped or "rolled" every few months to maintain its harsh texture. On the body and legs, the coat should be between ¼ to 1 inch in length on the bulk of the body and tail. The top of the head from back of the eyebrows to the base of the skull is tight. The throat and cheek area is short. Longer rectangular beard with medium lengths triangular brows. Tidy hocks and feet with shears.

Breed Facts & Characteristics

Country of Origin: *Scotland*

Height at Shoulder: *8"–11"*

Coat Length/Type: *Hard/Wiry*

Color: *Dark bluish black to light silvery gray or reddish brown to pale fawn.*

Correct grooming procedure:
Hand-Strip

Common pet grooming practices:
Clipper-Trim/Hand-Strip

-The Goal-
This breed is low slung with a curvy outline. The head is large and round. The front feet are larger than the back feet, representing a digging terrier. Back coat should be harsh, furnishings much softer and lighter in color.

Head is very full and round. Stop is deep. Eyes are round and looking straight forward.

Correctly Groomed: Hand-Stripped
Typical blades used on the body for pet grooming: #7F, #5F, #4F or shorter guard comb or a combination of those blades. Card coat after clipping to help maintain correct coat texture and color.

Scissor

Tail like a curved saber knife.

Scissor

Ears are tasseled.

Pattern lines are invisible on body.

Legs are straight and parallel.

Trim nails.

Rump is tight and clean showing off a well angulated rear assembly with strong thighs.

Scissor

Scissor

Scissor

Hocks are well let down.

The curved topline and the undercarriage line run in parallel curves.

Feet are tight and round. Front feet larger than rear feet.

General Description

This is a long, low athletic little dog with a curvy outline. The body of the dog is toned and flexible. The topline and the undercarriage line mimic one another in their outline. The legs are furnished with moderate feathering and the tail looks like a curved saber. The head is large and round, covered with silky hair. The eyes are full and round with a soft expression. The ears are tasseled.

Head Study — Dandie Dinmont Terrier

Head is unique with full round shape and tasseled ears. Eyes are large, round and face forward under a deep set brow. Look should be soft, expression wise and thoughtful. Topknot and muzzle are scissored large for the size but neat.

The line at the back of the skull is about an inch beyond the occiput

Fluff the topknot and scissor the head round and very full. The longer hair drapes over the ears and back of skull neatly.

Use a #10 or #15 blade on the outside of the ear, a #40 blade can be used on the inside of the ear leather with a very light touch. Remove "diamonded" shaped areas of fur on both the front and back edge of the ear leather. Let the longer coat of the topknot drape over the clipped area. The tassel covers the bottom ⅓ to ¼ of the ear tip. Edge the ear with small detailing shears. The ear is low set, roughly in line with the eye.

Comb the topknot forward, over the brows. With curved shears in reverse, trim a frame around the eye area. The line is steeply beveled, creating a deep set eye. Finish by softening the line with thinning shears.

Remove long hair from the stop area and bridge of nose before trimming the topknot.

The lower line of the head completes the circle that puts the eyes and nose at the center of the head piece when looking at the pet from the front. The lower line parallels the jaw bone. Comb all the coat down and trim with shears in a curved line running from the nose all the way up to behind the occiput. Soften the line with thinning shears to complete the head piece.

The triangular tassel blends with the level of the line of the jaw.

Throat is clipped with a blade slightly shorter than that used on the body, in a "U" shape, about 2–3 finger widths from breast bone.

Ear Safety Tip: Remember, always keep the tips of the shears towards the tips of the ears when edging for safety.

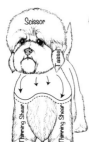

Head is large and covered with silky fur. The eyes look forward. Ears are tasseled. From the front and rear, the legs drop in straight, parallel lines from well-toned shoulders and thighs. When setting the pattern, use the turn of the muscles to set the lines. Rear is short, tight and clean. Leg furnishings are slightly longer than the body coat. Tail is feathered lightly in the shape of a curved saber.

Breed Facts & Characteristics

Country of Origin: *England*

Height at Shoulder: *15"–17"*

Coat Length/Type: *Combination/Silky*

Color: *The most common coat color is white and liver or white and black. Other acceptable colors, but not nearly as common, are tricolored with black and white or liver and white with tan points and blue or liver roans.*

Correct grooming procedure:
Card & Hand-Strip

Common pet grooming practices:
Clipper-Trim/Hand-Strip

-The Goal-
The coat should be fresh smelling, light and shiny. The natural body jacket should lay tight to the body. If clipping, no clipper marks. No loose hair or tangles left in the coat.

Coat on top of head lies smoothly.

Use a damp towel to go over muzzle after bathing.

Clip the top ⅓ of the ear or to the jawline.

Clip muzzle only if needed.

Throat area is thinned or left natural for pets.

The top of the front leg and the chest area should be separate areas.

Front of leg is short and smooth.

BLENDING AREA

Correctly Groomed: Hand-Strip
Typical blades used on the body for pet grooming: #7F, #5F, #4F, shorter guard combs, or a combination of those blades.
Card coat after clipping.

Tidy underside of the tail.

Bulk thin the thigh area to accentuate the muscle.

Leave furnishings long on back of thighs.

Shave pads. Trim the feet to appear neat and natural.

Neaten hocks.

The coat should look as natural as possible and all transitional pattern lines should be invisible.

General Description

The English Cocker Spaniel is a highly energetic, enthusiastic gun dog of classic good looks. A well-balanced, firmly built dog with great endurance. Chest is deep, reaching to the elbows. Topline is level or slightly sloping. Docked tail is an extension of the topline. Head is well-balanced and fine, blending smoothly between areas. Ears are long and the expression soft, kind and intelligent. The coat of an English Cocker Spaniel is soft and silky. They come in a number of color combinations. The jacket coat should lay smoothly over the head, throat, neck, shoulders, back, down the sides of the dog and the thighs. There is longer feathering on the ears, chest, undercarriage, belly and back of the legs.

Coat on the head lies smoothly. Finger pluck or thinning shear long strays if light coated. For heavier coated dogs, clip the cheeks and top of the head with blades ranging from a #7F to a #4F, used with or against the grain.

Remove whiskers only if the client requests or the muzzle needs to be clipped. Clip edges of lips with a #15 blade.

Clip top ⅓ of ear leather or to the jawline, if the ears are very long, with a #10 or #15 blade, creating a soft dip at the blending line. Neaten the clipped edge of the front of the ear with small shears. Neaten bottom of ear feathering so it's rounded and near.

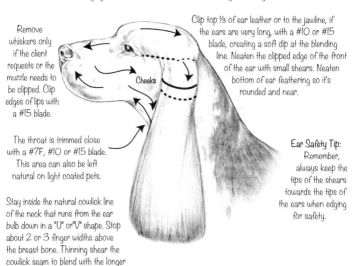

Cheeks

The throat is trimmed close with a #7F, #10 or #15 blade. This area can also be left natural on light coated pets.

Stay inside the natural cowlick line of the neck that runs from the ear bulb down in a "U" or "V" shape. Stop about 2 or 3 finger widths above the breast bone. Thinning shear the cowlick seam to blend with the longer coat of the neck.

Ear Safety Tip:
Remember, always keep the tips of the shears towards the tips of the ears when edging for safety.

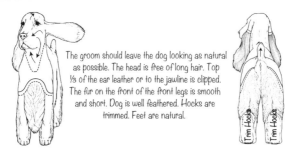

The groom should leave the dog looking as natural as possible. The head is free of long hair. Top ⅓ of the ear leather or to the jawline is clipped. The fur on the front of the front legs is smooth and short. Dog is well feathered. Hocks are trimmed. Feet are natural.

Trim Hocks

Breed Facts & Characteristics

Country of Origin: *England*

Height at Shoulder: *24"–25"*

Coat Length/Type: *Combination/Silky*

Color: *Background color always white with black, blue, red, liver or spots and flecking. Tricolors also acceptable.*

Correct grooming procedure:
Card & Hand-Strip

Common pet grooming practices:
Clipper-Trim/Hand-Strip

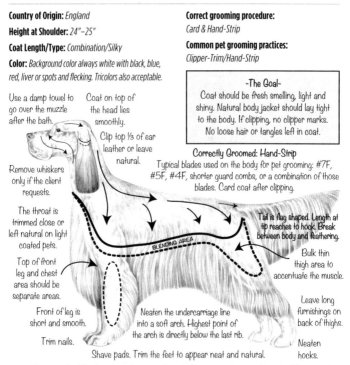

-The Goal-
Coat should be fresh smelling, light and shiny. Natural body jacket should lay tight to the body. If clipping, no clipper marks. No loose hair or tangles left in coat.

Correctly Groomed: Hand-Strip
Typical blades used on the body for pet grooming: #7F, #5F, #4F, shorter guard combs, or a combination of those blades. Card coat after clipping.

Use a damp towel to go over the muzzle after the bath.

Coat on top of the head lies smoothly.

Clip top ⅓ of ear leather or leave natural.

Remove whiskers only if the client requests.

The throat is trimmed close or left natural on light coated pets.

Top of front leg and chest area should be separate areas.

Front of leg is short and smooth.

Trim nails.

BLENDING AREA

Tail is flag shaped. Length at tip reaches to hock. Break between body and feathering.

Bulk thin thigh area to accentuate the muscle.

Leave long furnishings on back of thighs.

Neaten hocks.

Neaten the undercarriage line into a soft arch. Highest point of the arch is directly below the last rib.

Shave pads. Trim the feet to appear neat and natural.

The coat should look as natural as possible and all transitional pattern lines should be invisible.

General Description

The English Setter is a gun dog of great style and beauty. Is well-balanced, moderate in size. Chest is deep, reaching to the elbows. Topline is level or slightly sloping. Tail is an extension of topline, with no dip or break at the junction point. Tail is shaped like a flag and reaches to the hock when the dog is relaxed. Head is long and slender. The coat of an English Setter is soft, silky and speckled in color. Base color is always white with flecking, or roaning, in varying shades. Jacket coat should lay smoothly over the head, throat, neck, shoulders, back, down the sides of the dog and the thighs. Longer furnishings on ears, chest, undercarriage, belly, back of the legs and tail.

Coat on the head lies smoothly. Finger pluck or thinning shear long strays if light coated. Follow with carding and thinning. For heavier coated dogs, clip the cheeks and top of the head with blades ranging from a #7F to a #4F, used with or against the grain.

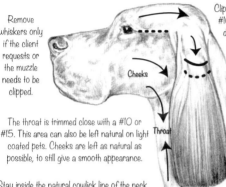

Remove whiskers only if the client requests or the muzzle needs to be clipped.

Cheeks

Clip top ⅓ of the ear leather with a #10 or #15 blade, creating a soft dip at the blending line. Or, thinning shear the top of the ear if the dog is very light coated. Neaten bottom of ear feathering so it's rounded and neat. Do not clip inside the ear leather. Leave the top, front edge untrimmed, helping to create a soft expression.

Throat

The throat is trimmed close with a #10 or #15. This area can also be left natural on light coated pets. Cheeks are left as natural as possible, to still give a smooth appearance.

Stay inside the natural cowlick line of the neck that runs from the ear bulb down in a "U" or "V" shape. Stop about 3 or 4 finger widths above the breast bone. Thinning shear the cowlick seam to blend with the longer coat of the neck.

The groom should leave the dog looking as natural as possible. The head is free of long hair. Top ⅓ of the ear leather is clipped. The fur on the front of the front legs is smooth and short. Dog is well feathered. Tail is flag shaped and reaches to the hock. Hocks are trimmed. Feet are natural.

Trim tail to top of hocks

Trim Hocks

Breed Facts & Characteristics

Country of Origin: *England*

Height at Shoulder: *19"–20"*

Coat Length/Type: *Combination/Silky*

Color: *The most common coat color is white and liver or white and black. Other acceptable colors, but not nearly as common are tricolored with black and white or liver and white with tan points and blue or liver roans.*

Correct grooming procedure:
Card & Hand-Strip

Common pet grooming practices:
Clipper-Trim & Hand-Strip

-The Goal-
Coat should be fresh smelling, light and shiny. Natural body jacket should lay tight to the body. If clipping, no clipper marks. No loose hair or tangles left in coat.

Use a damp towel to go over muzzle after bathing.

Clip muzzle if needed.

The throat is trimmed close or left natural on light coated pets.

The top of the front leg and the chest should be separate areas.

Front of leg is short and smooth.

Shave pads. Trim the feet to appear neat and natural.

Coat on top of the head lies smoothly.

Clip top ⅓ of ear or to the jawline.

Correctly Groomed: Hand-Strip
Typical blades used on the body for pet grooming: #8.5, #7F, #5F, #4F, shorter guard combs, or a combination of those blades. Card coat after clipping.

Bulk thin the thigh area to accentuate the muscle.

Leave long furnishings on the back of the thighs.

BLENDING AREA

Neaten undercarriage line into a soft arch. Highest point of arch is directly below last rib.

Neaten hocks.

The coat should look as natural as possible and all transitional pattern lines should be invisible.

General Description

The English Springer Spaniel is a gun dog of classic good looks and versatility. Is well-balanced, medium in size. Chest is deep, reaching to the elbows. Topline is level or slightly sloping. Docked tail is an extension of topline. Head is well-balanced. Ears are long and expression soft and trusting. Coat is soft and silky. A number of color combinations, but most common are liver & white or black & white. Jacket coat should lay smoothly over head, throat, neck, shoulders, back, down the sides of the dog and the thighs. Longer feathering on ears, chest, undercarriage, belly and back of all the legs.

Coat on the head lies smoothly. Finger pluck or thinning shear long strays if light coated. For heavier coated dogs, clip the cheeks and top of the head with blades ranging from a #7F to a #4F, used with or against the grain.

Remove whiskers only if the client requests or the muzzle needs to be clipped.

Clip top ⅓ of ear leather or to the jawline if the ears are very long with a #10 or #15 blade, creating a soft dip at the blending line. Neaten the clipped edge of the front of the ear with small shears. Neaten bottom of ear feathering so it's rounded and neat.

Cheeks are left as natural as possible to give a smooth appearance.

The throat is trimmed close with a #7F, #10 or #15 blade. This area can also be left natural on light coated pets.

Ear Safety Tip: Remember, always keep the tips of the shears towards the tips of the ears when edging for safety.

Stay inside the natural cowlick line of the neck that runs from the ear bulb down in a "U" or "V" shape. Stop about 3 or 4 finger widths above the breast bone. Thinning shear the cowlick seam to blend with the longer coat of the neck.

The groom should leave the dog looking as natural as possible. The head is free of long hair. Top 1/3 of the ear leather or to the jawline is clipped. The fur on the front of the front legs is smooth and short. Dog is well feathered. Hocks are trimmed. Feet are natural.

Breed Facts & Characteristics

Country of Origin: *England*

Height at Shoulder: *14½"–15½"*

Coat Length/Type: *Hard/Wiry*

Color: *Predominantly white with some color.*

Correct grooming procedure:
Hand-Strip

Common pet grooming practices:
Clipper-Trim

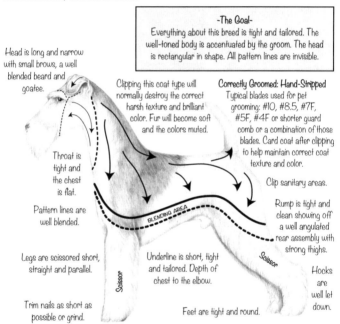

-The Goal-
Everything about this breed is tight and tailored. The well-toned body is accentuated by the groom. The head is rectangular in shape. All pattern lines are invisible.

Head is long and narrow with small brows, a well blended beard and goatee.

Clipping this coat type will normally destroy the correct harsh texture and brilliant color. Fur will become soft and the colors muted.

Correctly Groomed: Hand-Stripped
Typical blades used for pet grooming: #10, #8.5, #7F, #5F, #4F or shorter guard comb or a combination of those blades. Card coat after clipping to help maintain correct coat texture and color.

Throat is tight and the chest is flat.

Pattern lines are well blended.

Clip sanitary areas.

Rump is tight and clean showing off a well angulated rear assembly with strong thighs.

BLENDING AREA

Legs are scissored short, straight and parallel.

Underline is short, tight and tailored. Depth of chest to the elbow.

Scissor

Hocks are well let down.

Trim nails as short as possible or grind.

Feet are tight and round.

Scissor

General Description

The Wire Fox is tight and tailored. They are a square, well-balanced dog with a tendency to be leaner than some of the other long-legged terriers, but never racy. They have a sharp, keen expression that imparts the spirit and enthusiasm which runs in their blood. When grooming, remember there is nothing soft or fluffy about the breed. In the finished groom, there is very little coat hiding the contours of its body. The leg coat is slightly longer. The head is rectangular in shape with a piercing expression, moderate muzzle coat and small brows.

Head Study — Fox Terrier (Wire Haired)

Their expression is intelligent and energetic. The head is long, narrow and rectangular with small brows and a well blended beard and goatee. The top skull and the muzzle are equal in length with the stop area being the center point. All lines on the head are invisible.

Clip top skull with blades ranging from a #7F to a #5F, with the grain.

The eyebrows are very small, split at the stop area. There are no sharp lines. Shape and blend with thinning shears.

Use a #10 or #15 blade on the outside of the ear. A #40 blade can be used on the inside of the ear leather with a very light touch. Edge the ear with small detailing shears. The fold of the ear comes to well above the line of the top skull.

On the muzzle, hair is longer but not so long as to extend beyond planes of the top skull or cheeks. Blend the bulk of the muzzle with thinning shears or skim with a medium guard comb. Lightly trim the end of the muzzle to accentuate the rectangular head style. The lines at the side of the face are well blended and straight. Do not hollow out under the eye.

The throat is trimmed close with a #7F used against the grain or a #10 or #15 blade used with the coat growth.

Ear Safety Tip: Remember, always keep the tips of the shears towards the tips of the ears when edging for safety.

Labels on head illustration: Blend Well, Blend Well, Blend Well, Transitional Blending Area, Blend Well

Stay inside neck's natural cowlick line that runs from the ear bulb down in a "U" or "V" shape. Stop about 2 or 3 finger widths above breast bone. Thinning shear cowlick seam to blend with the longer coat of the neck.

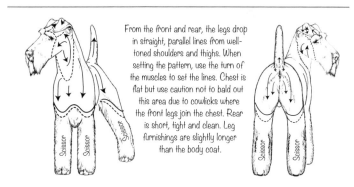

From the front and rear, the legs drop in straight, parallel lines from well-toned shoulders and thighs. When setting the pattern, use the turn of the muscles to set the lines. Chest is flat but use caution not to bald out this area due to cowlicks where the front legs join the chest. Rear is short, tight and clean. Leg furnishings are slightly longer than the body coat.

Labels on body illustrations: Scissor, Scissor, Scissor, Scissor, Scissor

Breed Facts & Characteristics

Country of Origin: *Germany*

Height at Shoulder: *23"–27"*

Coat Length/Type: *Hard/Wiry*

Color: *Salt and pepper or black.*

Correct grooming procedure:
Hand-Strip

Common pet grooming practices:
Clipper-Trim

-The Goal-
A tight and very tailored looking dog. Body is almost square in build with a rectangular head. When finished, pattern lines are invisible.

~Head Shape ~
Strong & Rectangular

Brows are long, arched triangles exposing a keen eye expression.

Ears trimmed very close.

~Pet Clipper-Trim~
Blade choices for bulk of the body range from a #10 to a #4F. Longer blade choices can be used in reversed for closer, super smooth results.

"Card" clippered body area to help promote proper coat growth and retain color.

Show off a powerful rear by accentuating a well angulated hind-end. Use the thigh muscle to set the pattern line.

Beard is left long and natural.

Use natural cowlick line to set neck pattern.

Chest is flat from profile. Watch for cowlicks.

Legs fall in parallel lines from the shoulder. Use the shoulder muscle to set pattern line.

Trim nails as close as possible or grind.

BLENDING AREA

Slight rise into the tuck-up area.

Brisket to elbow.

Scissor legs into columns.

Round feet.

Lowest point of pattern should be at bend.

Hocks are well let down.

Feet are rounded and face straight forward.

Pads are trimmed close.

General Description

The Giant Schnauzer is a powerful, muscular and squarely built dog of high energy and great intelligence. Its tail is docked short. It may have cropped or uncropped ears. When grooming, there is nothing soft or fluffy about this breed. In the finished groom, there is very little coat hiding the contours of its body. Leg coat and muzzle coat are slightly longer. The hallmark of the breed is its rectangular head, arched eyebrows and full mustache and beard.

Head Study

Shape the arched eyebrows by following the eye socket ridge. The stop area is clear, creating split brows. Use curved shears in reverse to help shape the eyebrows. The coat is very short at the back of the eye and gets longer towards the nose. Brow tips reach to the halfway point of the muzzle.

The beard and mustache form a rectangular head style. When viewed straight on, the cheeks and the beard should form one continuous line.

Cheeks and throat are smooth and clean. Blades ranging from a #10 to a #15, used with or against the grain, are common in pet styling. The line runs from the back corner of the eye to the cheek whisker nodule, to the chin nodule, up to the opposite cheek whisker nodule and opposite eye. Use the zygomatic arch to set the line from the back corner of the eye to the ear canal. The natural cowlick line assists with setting throat area. Create a soft "V" or "U" shape coming about 3–4 finger widths above the breast bone.

Hand-strip or clipper the top skull very close. If clipping, use blades ranging from a #10 used with the grain to a #4F used against the grain, depending on the coat density.

The ears may be cropped or natural. Either type is clipper-trimmed very close with blades ranging from a #10 or #15 on the outside and a #40 on the inside. Finish by edging the ears with small detailing shears keeping the tips of the shears towards the tips of the ears.

The occiput is the dividing line between the head and the neck.

At transition points on the body, blend the lines so they are invisible. Legs should be left fuller and fall into straight columns, from the body to the feet, on both the front and rear legs. The chest should be flat, but use caution not to bald out this area due to cowlicks found where the front legs meet the chest, on both the front and rear legs.

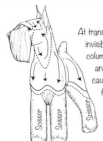

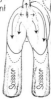

Breed Facts & Characteristics

Country of Origin: *Ireland*

Height at Shoulder: *12½"–14½"*

Coat Length/Type: *Hard/Wiry*

Color: *Wheaten, blue or brindle.*

Correct grooming procedure:
Hand-Strip

Common pet grooming practices:
Clipper-Trim /Hand-Strip

-The Goal-
A small, tough little terrier with a harsh outer coat, thick undercoat, and a natural head style with a rough and ready expression.

Head is left in its natural state with only light hand-stripping to tidy it up.

Ears are clipped close starting at the fold.

Correctly Groomed: Hand-Stripped
Typical blades used for pet grooming: #7F, #5F, #4F, or medium to longer guard combs, or a combination of those blades. Card coat after clipping to help maintain correct coat texture and color.

Coat on tail is the same as on the body.

Rump blends down into longer furnishings on the rear legs. No excessive coat hanging off rear end.

Throat is tight.

Pattern lines are well blended.

BLENDING AREA
Thinning Shear or Hand-Strip Furnishings

Coat on legs is left natural or feathered.

Underline is left longer. Lightly neaten line.

Feet are rounded. Front feet larger than rear feet.

Use a carding rake or stripping knife to remove undercoat and longer guard coat within the pattern area.

Trim nails as short as possible or grind.

General Description

This stout short-legged terrier sports the look of terriers from years gone by. The Glen possesses great strength and should always convey the impression of incredible power for the size of the dog. The breed is slightly longer than tall. The medium length coat is a combination of harsh outer coat and soft undercoat. Characteristic to this breed are rose or half-prick ears and bowed forequarters with turned out feet are typical traits of the breed. Tails may be docked or undocked.

The Glen of Imaal is a hardy terrier with ancient style. The head is powerful, strong and impressive for the size of the dog. Only very minor trimming is required to tidy up the head which is left in a very natural state.

Finger pluck or thinning shear only the longest hairs on the top of the head to accentuate a broad and slightly domed skull.

If the ear is lightly coated, hand-strip the outer ear leather or clip the ear with a #10 or #15 blade on the outside, a #40 on the inside.

Remove long hair from the stop area and bridge of nose before trimming the topknot.

The line at the back of the skull is about an inch beyond the occiput.

Clear stop area with thinners or by finger plucking only the coat that is irritating the eyes.

Lightly tidy the jawline with thinning shears.

Ear Safety Tip:
Remember, always keep the tips of the shears towards the tips of the ears when edging for safety.

Clip top ½ to ⅔ of ear or to fold.

The coat should look tidy but not sculpted. All lines are to be invisible. The ears can be rose or half-pricked. Clip the outer ½ to ⅔ tip only. Finger pluck or hand-strip the head furnishings to slightly tidy up the outline. Leave coat between the eyes in the stop area. If excessively long in the beard area, thinning shear the lower muzzle to neaten.

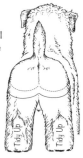

Breed Facts & Characteristics

Country of Origin: *Scotland*

Height at Shoulder: *23"–27"*

Coat Length/Type: *Combination/Silky*

Color: *Black with tan or mahogany points.*

Correct grooming procedure:
Card & Hand-Strip

Common pet grooming practices:
Clipper-Trim/Card & Hand-Strip

-The Goal-
Coat should be fresh smelling, light and shiny. Natural body jacket should lay tight to body. If clipping, no clipper marks. No loose hair or tangles left in coat.

Use a damp towel to go over the muzzle after the bath.

Coat on top of the head lies smoothly.

Clip top ⅓ of ear leather or trim to jawline.

Remove whiskers only if the client requests.

The throat is trimmed close or left natural on light coated pets.

Top of front leg and chest area should be separate areas.

Front of leg is short and smooth.

Trim nails.

Correctly Groomed: Hand-Strip
Typical blades used on pets: #7F, #5F, #4F, shorter guard combs, or a combination of those blades. Card coat after clipping.

Tail is flag shaped. Length at tip reaches to hock. Break between body and feathering.

Thin thigh area to accentuate the muscle.

Leave long furnishings on back of thighs.

Neaten hocks.

BLENDING AREA

Neaten undercarriage line into a soft arch. Highest point of arch is directly below last rib.

Shave pads. Trim the feet to appear neat and natural.

The coat should look as natural as possible and all transitional pattern lines should be invisible.

General Description

The Gordon Setter is a gun dog of great style and stamina. Well-balanced with excellent muscle tone and substantial bone. Chest is deep, reaching to the elbows. Topline is level or slightly sloping. Tail is an extension of topline, with no dip or break at the junction point. Tail is shaped like a flag and reaches to the hock when dog is relaxed. Head is deep and noble. Gordon Setter coat is black and tan in color. Texture is soft and silky. Jacket coat should lay smoothly over the head, throat, neck, shoulders, back, down the sides of the dog and the thighs. Longer furnishings on ears, chest, undercarriage, belly, back of the legs and tail.

Coat on the head lies smoothly. Finger pluck or thinning shear long strays if light coated. For heavier coated dogs, clip the cheeks and top of the head with blades ranging from a #7F to a #4F, used with or against the grain.

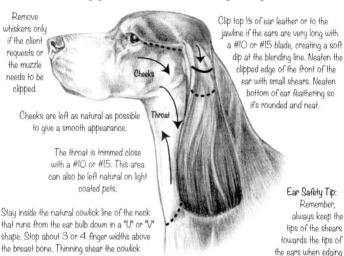

Remove whiskers only if the client requests or the muzzle needs to be clipped.

Clip top ⅓ of ear leather or to the jawline if the ears are very long with a #10 or #15 blade, creating a soft dip at the blending line. Neaten the clipped edge of the front of the ear with small shears. Neaten bottom of ear feathering so it's rounded and neat.

Cheeks

Throat

Cheeks are left as natural as possible to give a smooth appearance.

The throat is trimmed close with a #10 or #15. This area can also be left natural on light coated pets.

Ear Safety Tip: Remember, always keep the tips of the shears towards the tips of the ears when edging for safety.

Stay inside the natural cowlick line of the neck that runs from the ear bulb down in a "U" or "V" shape. Stop about 3 or 4 finger widths above the breast bone. Thinning shear the cowlick seam to blend with the longer coat of the neck.

The groom should leave the dog looking as natural as possible. The head is free of long hair. Tops of the ears are short. The fur on the front of the front legs is smooth and short. Dog is well feathered. Tail is flag shaped and reaches to the hock. Hocks are trimmed. Feet are natural.

Trim tail to top of hocks

Trim Hocks

Irish Red & White Setter

Breed Facts & Characteristics

Country of Origin: *Ireland*

Height at Shoulder: *22½"–26"*

Coat Length/Type: *Combination/Silky*

Color: *Base color white with clear patches of reds.*

Correct grooming procedure:
Card/Hand-Strip/Minor Trimming

Common pet grooming practices:
Card/Hand-Strip/Minor Trimming/Clipper-Cut

-The Goal-
Coat should be fresh smelling, light and shiny. Natural body jacket should lay tight to the body. No loose hair or tangles left in coat.

Use a damp towel to go over the muzzle after the bath.

Coat on top of the head lies smoothly.

Thinning shear top ¼ of the ear leather.

Correctly Groomed: Hand-Strip
Typical blades used on pets: #7F, #5F, #4F, shorter guard combs, or combo of those blades. Card coat after clipping.

Clip muzzle only if needed.

The throat is trimmed close or left natural on light coated pets.

Top of front leg and chest area should be separate areas.

Front of leg is short and smooth.

Trim nails as close as possible or grind.

BLENDING AREA

Tail is shaped like a flag. Length at tip reaches to hock.

Bulk thin thigh area to accentuate the muscle.

Leave long furnishings on back of thighs.

Neaten undercarriage line into a soft arch. Highest point of arch is directly below last rib.

Shave pads. Trim the feet to appear neat and natural.

Neaten hocks.

The coat should look as natural as possible and all transitional pattern lines should be invisible. Carding or raking out the loose body coat following the pattern outline for a natural look is preferred over clipping.

General Description

The Irish Red and White Setter is primarily an athletic field dog with great style. Is well-balanced and medium sized. Chest is deep, reaching to the elbow. Neck and back are strong. Topline from the withers to the croup is level. Croup is well rounded, sloping slightly downward to tail. Tail is shaped like a flag and reaches to the hock. Coat should lay smoothly over head, throat, neck, shoulders, back, down the sides of the dog and the thighs. Longer furnishings on ears, chest, undercarriage, belly and back of the thighs and tail are all moderate in length and density.

Coat on the head lies smoothly. Finger pluck or thinning shear long strays if light coated. Follow with carding and thinning. For heavier coated dogs, clip the cheeks and top of the head with blades ranging from a #7F to a #4F, used with or against the grain.

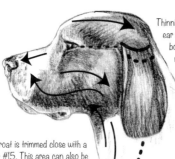

Remove whiskers only if the client requests or the muzzle needs to be clipped.

Thinning shear or clip the top ⅓ of the ear with a #10 or #15 blade. Neaten bottom of ear so it's rounded and neat. Do not clip the inside of ear leather. Leave the top, front edge untrimmed, helping to create a soft expression.

The throat is trimmed close with a #10 or #15. This area can also be left natural on light coated pets.

Stay inside the natural cowlick line of the neck that runs from the ear bulb down in a "U" or "V" shape. Stop about 3 or 4 finger widths above the breast bone. Thinning shear the cowlick seam to blend with the longer coat of the neck.

Ear Safety Tip: Remember, always keep the tips of the shears towards the tips of the ears when edging for safety.

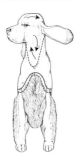

The groom should leave the dog looking as natural as possible. The head is free of long hair. Tops of the ears are short. The fur on the front of the front legs is smooth and short. Dog is well feathered. Tail is flag shaped and reaches to the hock. Hocks are trimmed. Feet are natural.

Trim tail to top of hocks.

Trim Hocks

Breed Facts & Characteristics

Country of Origin: *Ireland*

Height at Shoulder: *25"–27"*

Coat Length/Type: *Combination/Silky*

Color: *Deep, rich chestnut red or brown.*

Correct grooming procedure:
Card & Hand-Strip

Common pet grooming practices:
Clipper-Trim/Card & Hand-Strip

Use a damp towel to go over the muzzle after the bath.

Coat on top of the head lies smoothly.

Clip top ⅓ of ear leather, or jawline or leave natural.

Remove whiskers only if the client requests.

The throat is trimmed close or left natural on light coated pets.

Top of front leg and chest area should be separate areas.

Front of leg is short and smooth.

Trim nails.

-The Goal-
Coat should be fresh smelling, light and shiny. Natural body jacket should lay tight to body. If clipping, no clipper marks. No loose hair or tangles left in coat.

Correctly Groomed: Hand-Strip
Typical blades used on pets: #7F, #5F, #4F, shorter guard combs, or a combination of those blades. Card coat after clipping.

Tail is flag shaped. Length at tip reaches to hock. Break between body and feathering.

BLENDING AREA

Thin thigh area to accentuate the muscle.

Leave long furnishings on back of thighs.

Neaten hocks.

Neaten undercarriage line into a soft arch. Highest point of arch is directly below last rib.

Shave pads. Trim the feet to appear neat and natural.

The coat should look as natural as possible and all transitional pattern lines should be invisible.

General Description

The Irish Setter is a gun dog of great style and beauty. Is well-balanced, medium in size. Chest is deep, reaching to the elbows. Topline is level or slightly sloping. Tail is an extension of topline, with no dip or break at the junction point. Tail is shaped like a flag and reaches to hock when dog is relaxed. Head is long and slender. Coat is soft, silky and brilliant red in color. Jacket coat should lay smoothly over head, throat, neck, shoulders, back, down the sides of the dog and the thighs. Longer furnishings on ears, chest, undercarriage, belly, back of all the legs and tail.

Coat on the head lies smoothly. Finger pluck or thinning shear long strays if light coated. Follow with carding and thinning. The coat can change colors so dramatically on the Irish Setter, it is not recommended to clip the top of the head, even on pets. If clipping the body, then follow thorough with clipping the top of the head as well with a #7F, working with the lay of the coat.

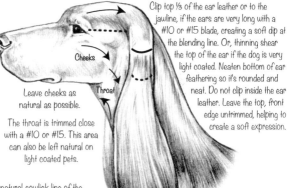

Clip top ⅓ of the ear leather or to the jawline, if the ears are very long with a #10 or #15 blade, creating a soft dip at the blending line. Or, thinning shear the top of the ear if the dog is very light coated. Neaten bottom of ear feathering so it's rounded and neat. Do not clip inside the ear leather. Leave the top, front edge untrimmed, helping to create a soft expression.

Remove whiskers only if the client requests or the muzzle needs to be clipped.

Cheeks

Leave cheeks as natural as possible.

Throat

The throat is trimmed close with a #10 or #15. This area can also be left natural on light coated pets.

Stay inside the natural cowlick line of the neck that runs from the ear bulb down in a "U" or "V" shape. Stop about 3 or 4 finger widths above the breast bone. Thinning shear the cowlick seam to blend with the longer coat of the neck.

Ear Safety Tip: Remember, always keep the tips of the shears towards the tips of the ears when edging for safety.

The groom should leave the dog looking as natural as possible. The head is free of long hair. Tops of the ears are short. The fur on the front of the front legs is smooth and short. Dog is well feathered. Tail is flag shaped and reaches to the top of the hock. Hocks are trimmed. Feet are natural.

Trim tail to top of hocks.

Trim Hocks

Breed Facts & Characteristics

Country of Origin: *Ireland*

Height at Shoulder: *18"*

Coat Length/Type: *Hard/Wiry*

Color: *Bright red, golden red, red wheaten or wheaten.*

Correct grooming procedure:
Hand-Strip

Common pet grooming practices:
Clipper-Trim/Hand-Strip

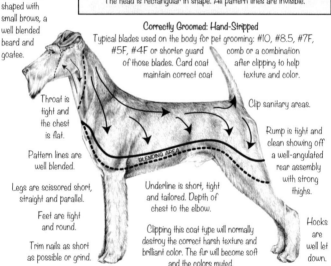

-The Goal-
Everything about this breed is tight and tailored. The well-toned body is accentuated by the groom. The furnishings on this breed are very short. The head is rectangular in shape. All pattern lines are invisible.

Head is brick shaped with small brows, a well blended beard and goatee.

Correctly Groomed: Hand-Stripped

Typical blades used on the body for pet grooming: #10, #8.5, #7F, #5F, #4F or shorter guard of those blades. Card coat maintain correct coat comb or a combination after clipping to help texture and color.

Throat is tight and the chest is flat.

Clip sanitary areas.

Rump is tight and clean showing off a well-angulated rear assembly with strong thighs.

Pattern lines are well blended.

BLENDING AREA

Legs are scissored short, straight and parallel.

Underline is short, tight and tailored. Depth of chest to the elbow.

Feet are tight and round.

Hocks are well let down.

Clipping this coat type will normally destroy the correct harsh texture and brilliant color. The fur will become soft and the colors muted.

Trim nails as short as possible or grind.

General Description

This breed is considered the sportsman of the long-legged terrier group. He is slightly longer than tall. The overall look is of a straightforward dog with a harsh coat that protects him from the elements. The jacket coat should be tight to the body with minimal leg furnishings. When grooming an Irish Terrier, remember there is nothing soft or fluffy about the breed. In the finished groom, *there is very little coat hiding the contours of any part of this dog.* The head is rectangular in shape with small brows, beard and a piercing expression.

Head Study

Their expression is alert, animated and friendly. Head is long and rectangular with small brows and a small, well blended beard and goatee. The top skull and the muzzle are equal in length with the stop area being the center point. All lines on the head are invisible.

Clip top skull with blades ranging from a #7F to a #5F, with the grain.

The eyebrows are very small, split at the stop area. There are no sharp lines. Shape and blend with thinning shears.

Use a #10 or #15 blade on the outside of the ear, a #40 blade can be used on the inside of the ear leather with a very light touch. Edge the ear with small detailing shears. The fold of the ear comes to just above the line of the top skull.

On the muzzle, the hair is longer but not so long as to extend beyond the planes of the top skull or cheeks. Blend the bulk of the muzzle with thinning shears or skim with a medium guard comb. Lightly trim the end of the muzzle to accentuate the rectangular head style. The lines at the side of the face are well blended and straight. Do not hollow out under the eye.

The throat is trimmed close with a #7F used against the grain or a #10 or #15 blade used with the coat growth.

Blend Well
Blend Well
Blend Well
Transitional Blending Area
Blend Well

Ear Safety Tip:
Remember, always keep the tips of the shears towards the tips of the ears when edging for safety.

Stay inside the natural cowlick line of the neck that runs from the ear bulb down in a "U" or "V" shape. Stop about 2 or 3 finger widths above the breast bone. Thinning shear the cowlick seam to blend with the longer coat of the neck.

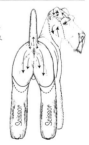

From the front and rear, the legs drop in straight, parallel lines from well-toned shoulders and thighs. When setting the pattern, use the turn of the muscles to set the lines. Chest is flat but use caution not to bald out this area due to cowlicks where the front legs join the chest. Rear is short, tight and clean. Leg furnishings are slightly longer than the body coat.

Scissor   Scissor   Scissor

Scissor   Scissor

Breed Facts & Characteristics

Country of Origin: *Ireland*

Height at Shoulder: *21"–24"*

Coat Length/Type: *Curly/Thick*

Color: *Solid liver color.*

Correct grooming procedure:
Hand-Scissor

Common pet grooming practices:
Clipper-Trim

-The Goal-
This breed has a coat that is highly distinguishable by the thick, curly brown coat. This feature is highly desirable when trimming. When finished, the coat should be fresh smelling, full of body and curly. No mats or tangles.

The topknot is left as natural as possible. It should be full of long, loose curls that cascade over the eyes, ears and occiput.

The throat and muzzle are clipped clean with close blades used in reverse.

A tuft of fur is left on the lower jaw just behind the lip line.

The blending areas should be invisible between body and legs.

The front legs are left fuller, dropping in straight, parallel lines.

Trim nails.

The ears are left full and natural.

Fur over the body may be left natural, trimmed with shears or longer guard combs. After trimming, misting the coat with water will restore any curl lost in the bathing and drying process.

Last ⅔ of tail is clipped close to create characteristic "rat-tail" look.

Blended, well angulated rear.

The rib cage is well rounded and the undercarriage is level.

This coat can easily be modified into a shorter trim version for a lower maintenance haircut while still retaining the essence of the proper breed profile.

Round the feet.

Hock are well let down.

BLENDING AREA

General Description

The Irish Water Spaniel is a breed that was developed to be a tough and rugged water dog. He is the largest of the spaniel breeds. His coat and overall look are unique with a thick curly brown coat, long ears, clean face and rat tail.

Head Study

Irish Water Spaniel

The lines for clipping the face start at the opening of the ear canal, in a straight line riding the bone to the back corner of the eye. Proceed under the eye, down the muzzle and clearing the stop area.

The throat and muzzle are clipped clean with close blades used in reverse. Typical blades are a #7F, #10 or a #15 blade.

Traditionally, a tuft of fur is left at the base of the jaw just before it meets the throat. The goatee should hang from the jaw line. It is important that it not come from the throat area. This tuft protects the area while retrieving ducks while hunting.

The throat will be "U" shaped starting at the base of the ears. The lowest point will be about 4 finger widths above the breast bone.

The topknot is left as natural as possible. It should be full of long, loose curls that cascade over the eyes, ears and occiput. Shape lightly with shears or thinning shears. After topknot is fully brushed out and shaped, spritz with water and scrunch the fur to bring the curls back into the hair.

The ears are left full and natural.

A unique feature of the Irish Water Spaniel is a tuft of fur left on the lower jaw. This tuft of fur is located on the jaw just ahead of the junction of the throat. It is a narrow tuft of fur hanging from the jaw but never comes beyond the back corners of the mouth. It is left long and natural, never hanging below the ears. It is there to protect the throat while working in the field.

Shape Lightly

Rat Tail

At transition points on the body, blend the lines so they are invisible. Legs should be left fuller and fall into straight columns, from the body to the feet on both the front and rear legs. The face is clean. A tuft of hair is left at the juncture of the jaw and throat. Topknot is a mass of curls that cascade over the head. Ears are long and natural. Coat is curly. Rat tail.

Scissor Full

Kerry Blue Terrier

Breed Facts & Characteristics

Country of Origin: *Ireland*

Height at Shoulder: *17½"–19½"*

Coat Length/Type: *Curly/Thick*

Color: *Blue gray or gray blue.*

Correct grooming procedure:
Hand-Scissor

Common pet grooming practices:
Clipper-Trim

-The Goal-
Highly stylized dog with unique curly coat. On finished trim, body coat remains curly while coat on legs & head is straight and full. Head is rectangular in shape with a fall of hair over the eyes. Mat free.

The top of the head is clipped very short with fall over the eyes, and long whiskers on the muzzle.

Correctly Groomed: Hand-Scissored
Typical blades used for pet grooming range from #7F, #5F, and #4F blades to a variety of guard combs or a combination of those trimming tools.

Thick carrot tail.

Throat is tight and the chest is flat.

Pattern lines are well blended on body, clearly defined on head and throat.

Clip sanitary areas.

Rump is tight and clean showing off a well angulated rear assembly with strong thighs.

Legs are scissored full, straight and parallel.

Underline is short and tailored. Depth of chest to the elbow.

Hocks are well let down.

Trim nails as short as possible or grind.

Feet are tight and round.

General Description

The Kerry is a medium sized, well-balanced dog with plenty of muscle, a rectangular head, well laid back shoulders and a short back. His coat is soft, thick and wavy. The color is always a blue gray in varying shades. His use as an all-around working and utility dog in his native land, which has created a versatile dog of true terrier style and spirit.

Head Study
Kerry Blue Terrier

Their expression is friendly but alert and keen. Head is rectangular with a long fall of hair over the stop area with a full beard and goatee. The top skull and the muzzle are equal in length with the stop area being the center point. All lines on the head are clean and sharp.

Clip top skull with blades ranging from a #7F to a #5F, used against the grain or blades ranging from a #10 to #7F with the grain.

The line for the fall follows the eye socket rim. Back corners of the eyes are trimmed closely to expose the eye. This line arches out towards the nose. It is crisp and clean.

On the muzzle, the hair is long and natural but does not break the line of the top skull. When combing down the beard, the lines at the side of the face form a straight plane. Just below the back corner of the eyes, the fur is short and well blended, creating fill under the eye. The clipper lines of the beard are clean and sharp.

The throat and cheeks are trimmed close with a #10 or #15 blade used against the grain.

Transitional Area

Use a #10 or #15 blade on the outside of the ear, a #40 blade can be used on the inside of the ear leather with a very light touch. Edge the ear with small detailing shears. The fold of the ear is level with the line of the top skull.

Ear Safety Tip:
Remember, always keep the tips of the shears towards the tips of the ears when edging for safety.

Stay inside the natural cowlick line of the neck that runs from the ear bulb down in a "U" or "V" shape. Stop about 2 or 3 finger widths above the breast bone. The line is very sharp and clean.

From the front and rear, the legs drop in straight, parallel lines from well-toned shoulders and thighs. When setting the pattern, use the turn of the muscles to set the lines. Chest is flat but use caution not to bald out this area due to cowlicks where the front legs join the chest. Rear is short, tight and clean. Leg furnishings are longer than the body coat.

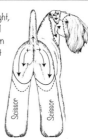

Breed Facts & Characteristics

Country of Origin: *Italy*

Height at Shoulder: *15½"–19½"*

Coat Length/Type: *Rustic/Curly*

Color: *Off white, orange or browns solid colors or off white with brown or orange spots. Roaning and/or limited white allowed.*

Correct grooming procedure:
Rake & Hand-Scissor

Common pet grooming practices:
Rake & Hand-Scissor

Either hand-scissor entire dog or clipper-trim to set basic pattern. Pet dogs can be modified into shorter trim styles using same basic pattern. Blenders and thinners work great.

-The Goal-
Coat is rustic and covers body with well-defined curls and springy ringlets. Looks somewhat rough and unkempt. Rake coat out prior to bathing. Air dry only.

No break at ears and domed head.

Deep-Set Eyes.

Ears are covered with longer coat and rounded to the length of the jawline.

Head is longer than body and roundish in shape.

Correctly Groomed:
Hand-scissored to 1½ to 2 inches all over. For pets; use a #5F, #4F or medium to longer guard combs to set the pattern on the bulk of the body.

Coat is curly—DO NOT BACKBRUSH

Throat and chest is trimmed slightly closer than body.

Tail reaches almost to the hock— shaped like an oversized carrot.

Pull an undercoat rake through the coat to remove dead undercoat prior to bathing.

Front and rear legs are about the same length as the bulk of the body—skim to same length as body—finish by hand with scissors or blenders.

Undercarriage is slightly shorter than body.

Backs of thighs can be shorter than body.

Hocks are parallel to ground.

Feet are rounded and face straight forward.

Pads are trimmed close.

Round feet.

General Description

The Lagotto is an active, medium sized dog with great eagerness for life. Originally bred as a water dog, but with its keen sense of smell, and strong ability for searching, it earned the job as a truffle hunter. It is a well-proportioned, squarely built dog with a round head and a long, carrot shaped tail. Rustic coated dogs *never* appear fluffy, polished or well groomed. Their coats are always air dried to maintain the springy curls characteristic of the breed.

Head is round and domed shape, slightly longer than the coat on the body.

Trim ears to the leather on the outside and lower edge—a bit longer next to the cheek so it blends seamlessly with the headpiece.

Use thinners, framing the eyes creating a beveled edge and a heavy brow.

No break in ears at skull junction.

Clear the inside corners of the eyes with thinners but leave coat on bridge of nose.

Layer length of coat on ears to blend with headpiece.

Blend head onto neck.

Trim off excessive coat that extends beyond the end of the muzzle.

Jaw rounded and to the length of the ear when dog is relaxed.

Slightly Shorter

Scissor　Scissor

There are only slight variations in coat length over the entire dog. The eyes and nose are at the center of the round head piece. Eyes are barely visible under a heavy brow. Ears blend with domed head and are level with the jaw. At transition points between the body and the legs, blend the lines so they are invisible. The legs are only a little longer in length than the body. They should fall into straight columns, to the rounded feet, when view from the front or rear. There are no breaks in the pattern anywhere on the dog. Tail shaped like a long carrot.

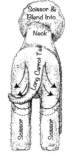

Scissor & Blend Into Neck

Long Carrot Tail

Scissor　Scissor

Breed Facts & Characteristics

Country of Origin: *England*

Height at Shoulder: *13½"–14½"*

Coat Length/Type: *Hard/Wiry*

Color: *Black, blue, liver, red and wheaten, wheaten or golden tan with blue, black, liver or grizzle saddle.*

Correct grooming procedure:
Hand-Strip

Common pet grooming practices:
Clipper-Trim/Hand-Strip

-The Goal-
Everything about the breed is tight and tailored. Grooming accentuates well-toned body. Head is rectangular in shape. All pattern lines are invisible.

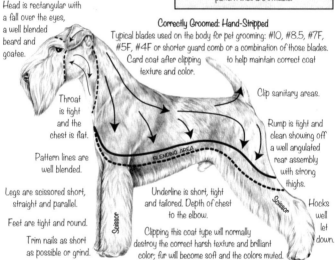

Head is rectangular with a fall over the eyes, a well blended beard and goatee.

Correctly Groomed: Hand-Stripped
Typical blades used on the body for pet grooming: #10, #8.5, #7F, #5F, #4F or shorter guard comb or a combination of those blades. Card coat after clipping to help maintain correct coat texture and color.

Clip sanitary areas.

Throat is tight and the chest is flat.

Rump is tight and clean showing off a well angulated rear assembly with strong thighs.

Pattern lines are well blended.

BLENDING AREA

Legs are scissored short, straight and parallel.

Feet are tight and round.

Trim nails as short as possible or grind.

Underline is short, tight and tailored. Depth of chest to the elbow.

Clipping this coat type will normally destroy the correct harsh texture and brilliant color; fur will become soft and the colors muted.

Hocks well let down.

Scissor

General Description

The Lakeland is the smallest of the long-legged terriers. They are a square, well-balanced dog. They have a sharp, keen expression that imparts the spirit and enthusiasm which runs in their blood. When grooming a Lakeland Terrier, remember there is nothing soft or fluffy about the breed. In the finished groom, there is very little coat hiding the contours of its body. The leg coat and muzzle coat are slightly longer. The head is rectangular in shape with a piercing expression and a fall of fur between the eyes.

Their expression is friendly but alert and bold. Head is brick shaped with a long fall of hair over the stop area with a well blended beard and goatee. The top skull and the muzzle are equal in length with the stop area being the center point. All lines on the head are heavily blended.

Clip top skull with blades ranging from a #7F to a #5F, with the grain.

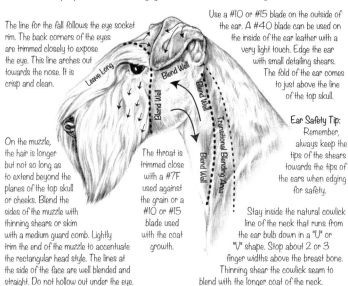

The line for the fall follows the eye socket rim. The back corners of the eyes are trimmed closely to expose the eye. This line arches out towards the nose. It is crisp and clean.

Use a #10 or #15 blade on the outside of the ear. A #40 blade can be used on the inside of the ear leather with a very light touch. Edge the ear with small detailing shears. The fold of the ear comes to just above the line of the top skull.

Ear Safety Tip:
Remember, always keep the tips of the shears towards the tips of the ears when edging for safety.

On the muzzle, the hair is longer but not so long as to extend beyond the planes of the top skull or cheeks. Blend the sides of the muzzle with thinning shears or skim with a medium guard comb. Lightly trim the end of the muzzle to accentuate the rectangular head style. The lines at the side of the face are well blended and straight. Do not hollow out under the eye.

The throat is trimmed close with a #7F used against the grain or a #10 or #15 blade used with the coat growth.

Stay inside the natural cowlick line of the neck that runs from the ear bulb down in a "U" or "V" shape. Stop about 2 or 3 finger widths above the breast bone. Thinning shear the cowlick seam to blend with the longer coat of the neck.

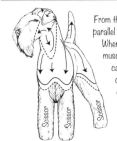

From the front and rear, the legs drop in straight, parallel lines from well-toned shoulders and thighs. When setting the pattern, use the turn of the muscles to set the lines. Chest is flat but use caution not to bald out this area due to cowlicks where the front legs join the chest. Rear is short, tight and clean. Leg furnishings are slightly longer coated than the body coat.

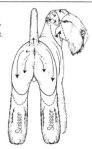

Löwchen

Breed Facts & Characteristics

Country of Origin: *Germany*

Height at Shoulder: *12"–14"*

Coat Length/Type: *Long/Flowing*

Color: *All colors and coat patterns are allowed.*

Correct grooming procedure:
Bathe & Brush Out/Clipper-Trim

Common pet grooming practices:
Bathe & Brush Out/Clipper-Trim

-The Goal-

Coat should be mat- and tangle-free. The fur should be light and airy, moving freely with the dog as it moves. Bare skin should be hair free and smooth. Pattern lines clean and crisp.

All long fur is to be left totally natural without any trimming.

The head is left in a natural state.

Line comb and line brush to remove any mats or tangles in the coat.

Front legs are clipped from the elbow to just above the pastern joint.

Trim nails as close as possible or grind.

Clip tail to about half way point of the tail bone leaving a plume on the end.

Clip rear section with blades ranging from a #7F or #15 blade, with or against the coat growth based on skin sensitivity. Use last rib, top of hock and top of knee to set pattern lines. All lines should be crisp and neat.

The cuffs should be equal in size and balanced, front to back.

Feet are clipped with a #10 or #15 up to the point where the dew claws have been removed. Shave the pads.

General Description

This breed was developed in the Pre-Renaissance time-period where ladies of the court had their dogs groomed to look like a little lion. This breed is an active, fun loving, small dog with great style. The coat of the head, ears, front portion of the dog and end of the tail are naturally long and flowing, never trimmed. The rear portion of the dog is clipped very close including half the tail and down just above the hocks. On the front legs, the forearm is also clipped close as well as all the feet. Tufts of fur are left around joints of the pasterns and hocks.

The head is left long and natural without any trimming

The longer coat around the head and chest is left long and natural. The rear is clipped with blades ranging from a #15 to a #7F in reverse. Begin the clipping work just above the hocks on the rear legs and clip to the last rib on the body. Clip half the tail, leaving a plume on the end. On the front legs, lift the longer coat out of the way and clip the top of the leg from just above the pastern to the elbow. The tops of all cuffs should be level with each other. Feet are clipped like a poodle.

Breed Facts & Characteristics

Country of Origin: *Germany*

Height at Shoulder: *12"–14"*

Coat Length/Type: *Hard/Wiry*

Color: *Salt and pepper, black and silver, or solid black.*

Correct grooming procedure:
Hand-Strip

Common pet grooming practices:
Clipper-Trim

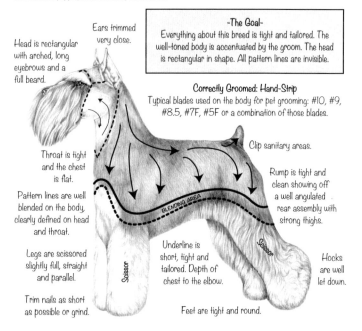

Ears trimmed very close.

Head is rectangular with arched, long eyebrows and a full beard.

-The Goal-
Everything about this breed is tight and tailored. The well-toned body is accentuated by the groom. The head is rectangular in shape. All pattern lines are invisible.

Correctly Groomed: Hand-Strip
Typical blades used on the body for pet grooming: #10, #9, #8.5, #7F, #5F or a combination of those blades.

Clip sanitary areas.

Throat is tight and the chest is flat.

Pattern lines are well blended on the body, clearly defined on head and throat.

Rump is tight and clean showing off a well angulated rear assembly with strong thighs.

BLENDING AREA

Legs are scissored slightly full, straight and parallel.

Underline is short, tight and tailored. Depth of chest to the elbow.

Scissor

Hocks are well let down.

Trim nails as short as possible or grind.

Scissor

Feet are tight and round.

General Description

The Miniature Schnauzer is a powerful, muscular and squarely built dog of high energy and great intelligence. Its tail is docked short. It may have cropped or uncropped ears. When grooming a Miniature Schnauzer, remember there is nothing soft or fluffy about the breed. In the finished groom, there is very little coat hiding the contours of its body. The leg coat and muzzle coat are slightly longer. The hallmark of the breed is its rectangular head, arched eyebrows and full mustache and beard.

Head Study   Miniature Schnauzer

Their expression is friendly but alert and bold. Head is rectangular with long, arched eyebrows and a full beard. The top skull and the muzzle are equal in length with the stop area being the center point. All lines on the head are clean and sharp.

Clip top skull with blades ranging from a #7F to a #5F, used against the grain or blades ranging from a #10 to #7F with the grain.

Use a # 10 or #15 blade on the outside of the ear, a #40 blade can be used on the inside of the ear leather with a very light touch. Edge the ear with small detailing shears.

The eyebrows are split, long and arched. The brows will be very short at the back corner of the eye.

The beard is long, full and natural. When combing down the beard, the lines at the side of the face form a straight plane. Just below the back corner of the eyes, the fur is short and well blended, creating fill under the eye. The clipper lines of the beard are clean and sharp.

The throat is trimmed close with a #7F used against the grain or a #10 or #15 blade used with the coat growth.

Clean & Sharp

Blend Well

Blend Well

Transitional Blending Area

Blend Well

Ear Safety Tip: Remember, always keep the tips of the shears towards the tips of the ears when edging for safety.

Stay inside natural cowlick line of the neck that runs from the ear bulb down in a "U" or "V" shape. Stop about 2 or 3 finger widths above breast bone. Thinning shear the cowlick seam to blend with the longer coat of the neck.

When setting the beard, use the back corners of the eyes and the whisker nodule on the cheeks and under the jaw as basic guidelines: "Connect the dots."

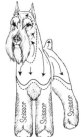

From the front and rear, the legs drop in straight, parallel lines from well-toned shoulders and thighs. When setting the pattern, use the turn of the muscles to set the lines. Chest is flat but use caution not to bald out this area due to cowlicks where the front legs join the chest. Rear is short, tight and clean. Leg furnishings are longer than the body coat.

Poodle

Breed Facts & Characteristics

Country of Origin: *Germany*

Height at Shoulder: *10"–25"*

Coat Length/Type: *Long/Curly*

Color: *All solid colors in shades of black, grays, browns, tans and white.*

Correct grooming procedure:
Hand-Scissor

Common pet grooming practices:
Clipper-Cut

-The Goal-
Longer fur should look cloud-like, void of any clipper or scissor marks. Close clipper work is smooth and even. Coat needs to be totally mat free. Outline should be velvet smooth and neat. Breed is squarely built, well-balanced and elegant.

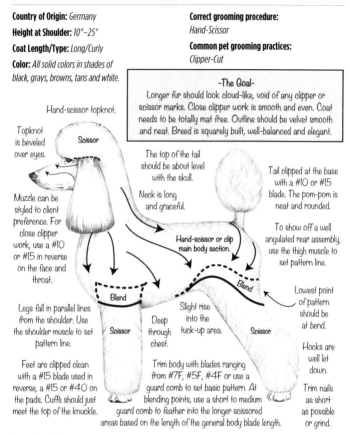

Hand-scissor topknot.

Topknot is beveled over eyes.

Scissor

Muzzle can be styled to client preference. For close clipper work, use a #10 or #15 in reverse on the face and throat.

The top of the tail should be about level with the skull.

Neck is long and graceful.

Tail clipped at the base with a #10 or #15 blade. The pom-pom is neat and rounded.

Hand-scissor or clip main body section.

To show off a well angulated rear assembly, use the thigh muscle to set pattern line.

Blend

Legs fall in parallel lines from the shoulder. Use the shoulder muscle to set pattern line.

Feet are clipped clean with a #15 blade used in reverse, a #15 or #40 on the pads. Cuffs should just meet the top of the knuckle.

Scissor

Deep through chest.

Slight rise into the tuck-up area.

Scissor

Blend

Lowest point of pattern should be at bend.

Hocks are well let down.

Trim nails as short as possible or grind.

Trim body with blades ranging from #7F, #5F, #4F or use a guard comb to set basic pattern. At blending points, use a short to medium guard comb to feather into the longer scissored areas based on the length of the general body blade length.

General Description

Poodles are stylish, squarely-built and very intelligent. They have an air of sophistication and distinction all to themselves. They are energetic, athletic and well-proportioned. Their structure allows for free, fluid and elegant movement in all their gaits. This breed's coat is considered non-shedding and hypo-allergenic.

Their expression is friendly, intelligent and alert. The rounded topknot accentuates this appearance and adds balance to the overall look. The top skull and the muzzle are equal in length with the stop area being the center point. The topknot is well shaped and neat.

Shape the topknot into a smooth, even extension of the skull. The clipper lines are crisp and clean. The longer coat is softly rounded with curved shears to create a well-balanced, neat topknot that balances with the overall length of the trim.

Bevel the topknot line steeply so it is very short right above the eyes, getting longer as it moves out and away from the eye.

Shape topknot in a rounded fashion. It should appear to be an extension of the skull and be in balance with the rest of the trim. The ideal height for the topknot is the distance measured between the outside corners of the eyes.

On a clean face, the muzzle is clipped very close. Use a #10 or #15 against the grain with a light touch. Clear the entire cheek, throat and muzzle area. The line for the topknot goes from the ear canal forward following the bony ridge straight to the back corner of the eye. Clip under the eye. At the stop area, clip out an inverted triangle and continue to clip right down the bridge of the nose. Stretch the skin of the lips while clipping to ensure they are clipped clean.

Once sides and front are trimmed, fluff entire topknot and round it out with curved shears. Blend the topknot into the neck.

Softly round the ends of the ears based on client preference.

Style Options:
Ear and mustache styles may be interchanged based on client preference.

Throat is clipped clean with same blade used on muzzle. Line will be from ear bulb to about 3–4 finger widths above breast bone. Neck is elegantly clipped in a "U" or "V" shape.

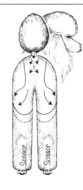

The neck line is clean, long and plunging. Cuff sits just on top of the knuckles. At transition points between the body and the legs, blend the lines so they are invisible. The legs should fall into straight columns, from the body to the cuffed feet, when viewed from the front or rear. The pom-pom on the tail is a well shaped oval.

Common Pet Poodle Trims

Pet grooming the poodle can unleash the creative spirit in many pet professionals. This seems to be one of the few purebreds where it is considered "acceptable" to have some fun with trim styles. The wide variety of sizes and colors and a coat type that lends itself to sculpture means the sky is the limit as to what may walk down the street.

These are ten of the more common trims on poodles. There are several more, but most are variations of these basic trims.

- *Retriever/All/Kennel*
- *Lamb/Bladed Body: Stylized Legs*
- *Puppy Cut*
- *Euro/German*
- *Single Banded*

- *Teddy Bear*
- *New Yorker/Double Banded*
- *Dutch*
- *Town & County*
- *Miami/Clown Cut*

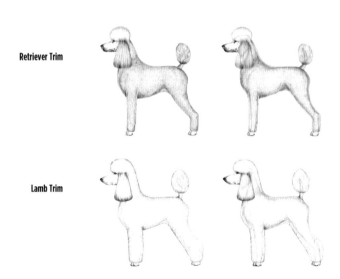

Retriever Trim

Lamb Trim

Puppy Cut

Euro or German Trim

Single Banded Trim

Teddy Bear Trim

New Yorker Trim

Dutch Trim

Town & Country Trim

Miami or Clown Trim

Non-Angled Mustache

Angled Mustache

Rounded Topknot with a Clean Face

Rounded Topknot with a German Mustache

Straight-Sided Topknot with a Donut Mustache

Flared Topknot with a Small Mustache

Small Flared Topknot with a French Mustache

Breed Facts & Characteristics

Country of Origin: *Portugal*

Height at Shoulder: *17"–23"*

Coat Length/Type: *Curly/Thick or Wavy/Long*

Color: *Black, white and all shades of brown. The black or browns can be combined with white for a two color dog.*

Correct grooming procedure:
Hand-Scissor

Common pet grooming practices:
Clipper-Trim

> -The Goal-
> The coat is full of body and perfectly fluffed out. Well-balanced. Totally mat free. No scissor marks in coat.

Either hand-scissor entire dog or use guard comb to set basic pattern. Pet dogs can be modified into shorter trim styles using same basic pattern.

~Wavy Coated Variety~
Same Trim Pattern

Hand-scissor top of head.

Head is broad and rounded.

Muzzle is wedge shaped. Hand-scissor or use a blade ranging from a #5F to a medium length guard comb.

Legs fall in parallel lines from the shoulder. Use the shoulder muscle to set pattern line.

Feet are rounded and face straight forward.

Trim nails as close as possible or grind.

Ears are heart shaped and level with jaw line.

Neck is short and powerful. Leave a little longer than body.

~Working Retriever Trim~
Curly Coated

Leave a natural tuft on the end of the tail.

Show off a powerful rear by accentuating a well angulated hind-end. Use the thigh muscle to set the pattern line.

Lowest point of pattern should be at bend.

Hocks are well let down.

Pads are trimmed close.

BLEND

BLEND

Slight rise into tuck-up area.

Scissor legs into columns.

Round feet.

General Description

The Portuguese Water Dog is an active, robust water dog developed to assist fishermen off the shores of Portugal. It is tough and highly intelligent. It is a medium-sized working dog, slightly longer than it is tall at the withers. Head is broad, ears heart-shaped, short neck and the feet webbed. It has good substance with a muscular body.

Working Retriever Trim

~Curly Coated Variety~

The topknot is trimmed to blend with the body coat. The stop area is deep set. The coat above the eye is beveled into the topknot to create a deep set eye.

The ears are heart shaped without any break from the topknot to the ear leather. The ear is covered with about 1 to 2 inches of fur which can be feathered in by using a long guard comb over a #40 blade to set the length or scissor by hand. Trim the bottom of the ear level with the jaw line.

The muzzle area may be clipper-cut with a #4F or #5F blade or scissor-trimmed by hand. The shape of the muzzle is a wedge, tighter at the nose and broadening out towards the cheeks.

~Wavy Coated Variety~

At transition points between the body and the legs, blend the lines so they are invisible. The legs should fall into straight columns, from the body to the rounded feet, when viewed from the front or rear.

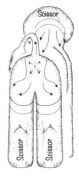

Lion Trim in General

On both the curly and wavy coat types, either trim style is acceptable. However, it is most common to see curly coated dogs sporting the Working Retriever trim style while wavy coated dogs are most commonly found in the Lion Trim.

~Curly Coated Variety~
Same Trim Pattern

-The Goal-
The pattern lines are crisp and clean. The coat is wavy and full of body. The coat floats with the dog as it moves.

Either hand-scissor the longer areas of the dog or use a long guard comb to set the basic pattern. Pet dogs can be modified into shorter trim styles using the same basic pattern.

Thinning shears work great with this coat type to soften and blend the coat. They are erasers for any sharp marks in the coat left from scissors or clippers.

Head is broad and rounded.

Muzzle is clipped close with blades ranging from a #7F to a #15, used either with the coat growth or against, based on skin sensitivity and client preference.

Hand-scissor top of head.

Ears are heart shaped.

Using the same blade as on the rear, clip the tail—leaving 1/3 to 1/2 at the end—to create a natural tuft.

Neck is short and powerful. Leave a little longer than body.

Pattern line goes to last two ribs. Rear assembly is clipped with blades ranging from a #4F to as short as a #10, used either with or against the grain of the coat.

Legs fall in parallel lines from the shoulder. Use the shoulder muscle to set pattern line.

BLEND

Feet are rounded and face straight forward.

Deep through chest.

Scissor legs into straight columns.

Double check between toes for long hair.

Pads are trimmed close.

Trim nails as close as possible or grind.

Lion Trim

~Wavy Coated Variety~

The topknot is trimmed to blend with the body coat. The stop area is deep set. The coat above the eye is beveled into the topknot to create a deep set eye.

The ears are heart shaped without any break from the topknot to the ear leather. The ear is covered with about 1 to 2 inches of fur which can be feathered in by using a long guard comb over a #40 blade to set the length, or scissor by hand. Trim the bottom of the ear level with the jaw line.

The muzzle area is clipper-cut with blades ranging from a #4 to a #10 blade. Clip the entire muzzle and jaw. Do not clip back to the ear canal or down throat.

~Curly Coated Variety~

At transition points between the body and the front legs, blend lines so they are invisible. The front legs should fall into straight columns, from the body to the rounded feet, when viewed from the front or rear.

Clip hindquarters with blades ranging from a #10 to a #4F so it is smooth and even. Tidy around feet with shears or blenders.

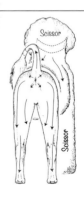

Breed Facts & Characteristics

Country of Origin: *Hungary*

Height at Shoulder: *15"–18½"*

Coat Length/Type: *Rustic/Curly*

Color: *Any solid shade of white, cream, fawn, gray or black. Tan or gray colored dogs may have limited darker shading. Small white patch acceptable on chest and toes.*

Correct grooming procedure:
Rustic Hand-Scissored

Common pet grooming practices:
Rustic Hand-Scissored/Clipper-Trim

-The Goal-
Coat is rustic and covers body with well-defined curls and springy ringlets. Looks rough and unkempt. Rake coat out prior to bathing. Air dry only.

Either hand-scissor or clipper-trim to set basic pattern. Pet dogs can be modified into shorter trim styles using same basic pattern. Blenders and thinners work great.

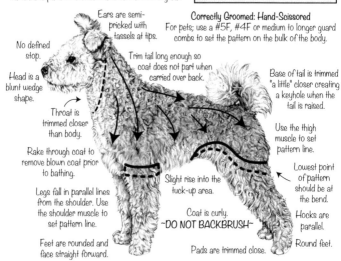

Correctly Groomed: Hand-Scissored
For pets; use a #5F, #4F or medium to longer guard combs to set the pattern on the bulk of the body.

Ears are semi-pricked with tassels at tips.

No defined stop.

Head is a blunt wedge shape.

Trim tail long enough so coat does not part when carried over back.

Base of tail is trimmed "a little" closer creating a keyhole when the tail is raised.

Throat is trimmed closer than body.

Use the thigh muscle to set pattern line.

Rake through coat to remove blown coat prior to bathing.

Lowest point of pattern should be at the bend.

Legs fall in parallel lines from the shoulder. Use the shoulder muscle to set pattern line.

Slight rise into the tuck-up area.

Coat is curly.
~DO NOT BACKBRUSH~

Hocks are parallel.

Round feet.

Feet are rounded and face straight forward.

Pads are trimmed close.

General Description

An active, intelligent medium sized dog with great enthusiasm for life. A versatile stock dog developed to herd and drive all types of livestock. Is relatively lean and squarely built dog. Coats are considered rustic and double coated—a curly combination of soft undercoat and harsh guard hair. They have a unique wedge shaped head with a semi-pricked ear and a whimsical expression. Long tail curls over their backs. Rustic coated dogs *never* appear fluffy, polished or well groomed. Coats are always air dried to maintain the springy curls characteristic of the breed.

Unique head shaped like a blunt wedge: narrower at the nose—widening out at cheeks and over topskull. No definition between eyes at the stop. Ears are high-set and tasseled. Expression is bright and whimsical.

Ears are semi-pricked with Bedlington-type tassels at the tips.

Stop is level—expose eye with thinners, trimming just over each eye, beveling the shears on a diagonal to create a deep-set eye.

Trim longer coat from the end of the muzzle extending beyond the nose.

Before scissoring in the wedged line on sides of the head, trim cheeks between ½ and 1 inch in length to establish shape and set a trimming target.

With long, straight shears or large thinners, block in a straight line from the nose to the back-skull to start the wedge shape.

On outside of the ear leather, shorten fur with thinners leaving a generous longer tassel on the ear tip (from the fold to the tip of the leather). Slightly round the shape of the scissored tassel.

Trim coat short around ear base to accentuate a high-set ear.

Remove longer hair from the inside of the ear leather with shears or thinners to remove weight.

Coat on lower jaw will be about ¾ to 1 inch in length—scissor straight back from the muzzle to the throat.

Throat is shorter starting under the base of the ears, dropping to a few fingers above the breast bone.

Do not straighten coat—use a wide-toothed comb sparingly to double check work.

Wedge Shape

Scissor　　Scissor

There are only slight variations in coat length over the entire dog. The head is wedge shaped. The ears are styled into overgrown tasseled Bedlington-type ears. At transition points between the body and the legs, blend the lines so they are invisible. The legs are only a little longer in length than the body. They should fall into straight columns, to the rounded feet, when viewed from the front or rear. There are no breaks in the pattern anywhere on the dog. Tail coat is slightly longer than the body and never so long that it parts when carried over the back.

Overgrown Bedlington-Type Ears

Scissor　　Scissor

Scottish Terrier

Breed Facts & Characteristics

Country of Origin: *Scotland*

Height at Shoulder: *9½"–10½"*

Coat Length/Type: *Hard/Wiry*

Color: *Black, wheaten or brindled of any color.*

Correct grooming procedure:
Hand-Strip

Common pet grooming practices:
Clipper-Trim

-The Goal-
Everything about this breed is compact and tailored. The muscular body is accentuated by the groom. The head is rectangular in shape with long arched eyebrows and tufted ears. Pattern lines on the body are invisible; on the head, crisp and clean.

Ears have tufts in front of ear canal opening.

Head is rectangular with arched, long eyebrows and a full beard and goatee.

Correctly Groomed: Hand-Stripped

Typical blades used on the body for pet grooming: #8.5, #7F, #5F, #4F or shorter or a combination of those blades. Card maintain correct coat

guard comb or a combination coat after clipping to help texture and color.

Carrot Tail.

Rump blends down into longer furnishings on the rear legs. No excessive coat hanging off rear end.

Throat is tight.

Pattern lines are well blended on body, clearly defined on head and throat.

Hocks are well let down.

BLENDING AREA

Chest is pronounced and covered with long feathers.

Coat on legs is left natural or feathered.

Trim nails as short as possible or grind.

Underline is left long. Lightly neaten line.

Feet are rounded. Front feet are larger than rear feet.

General Description

This is a compact, very powerful little dog that is very stylish and tailored. The top section shows off a broad, toned body while the lower section is feathered. The head is rectangular with accentuated long eyebrows, pricked ears with small tufts of fur at the inner base and a full beard. The expression is piercing, full of purpose and vigor.

Head Study

Scottish Terrier

Expression is keen, alert and bold. Narrow rectangular head with long, arched eyebrows and full beard. Top skull and muzzle are equal in length with the stop area being the center point. All lines on the head are clean and sharp.

Ear Safety Tip: Always keep tips of the shears towards tips of the ears when edging.

Clip the top skull with blades ranging from a #5F to a #4F, used against the grain or blades from a #10 to #7F with the grain.

Eyebrows are split, long and arched. Brows will be very short at back eye corner.

Beard is long, full and natural. When combing beard down, lines at the side of the face form a straight plane. Just below back corner of the eyes, fur is short and well blended, creating fill under the eye. The clipper lines of the beard are clean and sharp.

The throat and cheeks are trimmed close with a #7F used against the grain or a #10 or #15 blade, used with the coat growth.

Ears have small triangular tufts at the base of the front. Almost the entire back of ear is clipped with a #10 or #15 blade. The inside 1/3 of the ear tip is clipped clean. Detail outer ear leather edge from base to tip with small detailing shears. Edge only top 1/3 of ear leather on inside tip. Shape tufts with thinning shears.

Beard line runs from back eye corners to back mouth corner. To form goatee: On lower jaw, lift up beard and continue clipping lower jaw, about 1" from back mouth corner.

Stay inside neck's natural cowlick line that runs from ear bulb down in a "U" or "V" shape. Stop about 2 or 3 finger widths above breast bone. Thinning shear cowlick seam to blend with longer neck coat.

Transitional Area

The head is long and rectangular with long, split arched eyebrows and tufts at the base of the ears. From the front and rear, the legs drop in straight, parallel lines from well-toned shoulders and thighs. When setting the pattern, use the turn of the muscles to set the lines. Under the tail is short and clean with a drape of longer fur covering the back of the thighs. Leg furnishings are longer than the body coat. Tail is carrot shaped and very short on the back side.

Leave Tuft

Thinning Shear

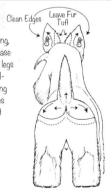

Clean Edges   Leave Fur Tuft

Clip   Clip

Breed Facts & Characteristics

Country of Origin: *Wales*

Height at Shoulder: *10"–11"*

Coat Length/Type: *Hard/Wiry*

Color: *All white, or with lemon, tan or badger markings.*

Correct grooming procedure:
Hand-Strip

Common pet grooming practices:
Clipper-Trim

-The Goal-
Everything about this breed is compact and tailored. The muscular body is accentuated by the groom. The head is rectangular in shape with a long fall of hair between the eyes. Pattern lines on the body are invisible, on the head, they are crisp and clean.

Head is rectangular with a fall over the eyes, a long beard and goatee.

Ears are clipped short.

Correctly Groomed: Hand-Stripped

Typical blades used on the body for pet grooming: #8.5, #7F, #5F, #4F or shorter guard comb or a combination of those blades. Card coat after clipping to help maintain correct coat texture and color.

Tail same length as body.

Throat is tight.

BLENDING AREA

Hocks are well let down.

Pattern lines are well blended on body; clearly defined on head and throat.

Thinning Shear

Thinning Shear

Chest is pronounced and covered with long feathers.

Coat on legs is left natural or feathered.

Trim nails as short as possible or grind.

Underline is left long. Lightly neaten line.

Feet are rounded. Front feet are larger than rear feet.

General Description

This is a compact, very powerful little dog that also is very stylish and tailored. The top section shows off a toned body while the lower section is feathered. The head is rectangular, accentuated with a fall of hair over the eyes and a full beard. The expression is piercing, full of purpose and vigor.

Their expression is friendly but alert and bold. Head is rectangular with a long fall of hair over the stop area with a full beard and goatee. The top skull and the muzzle are equal in length with the stop area being the center point. All lines on the head are clean and sharp.

Clip top skull with blades ranging from a #7F to a #5F, used against the grain or blades ranging from a #10 to #7F with the grain.

The line for the fall follows the eye socket rim. The back corners of the eyes are trimmed closely to expose the eye. This line arches out towards the nose. It is crisp and clean.

On the muzzle, the hair is long and natural but does not break the line of the top skull. When combing down the beard, the lines at the side of the face form a straight plane. Just below the back corner of the eyes, the fur is short and well blended, creating fill under the eye. The clipper lines of the beard are clean and sharp.

Leave Long

Clean & Sharp

Blend Well

Transitional Blending Area

Blend Well

The throat is trimmed close with a #7F used against the grain or a #10 or #15 blade used with the coat growth.

Use a #10 or #15 blade on the outside of the ear. A #40 blade can be used on the inside of the ear leather with a very light touch. Edge the ear with small detailing shears. The fold of the ear is level with the line of the top skull.

Ear Safety Tip:
Remember, always keep the tips of the shears towards the tips of the ears when edging for safety.

Stay inside the natural cowlick line of the neck that runs from the ear bulb down in a "U" or "V" shape. Stop about 2 or 3 finger widths above the breast bone. Thinning shear the cowlick seam to blend with the longer coat of the neck.

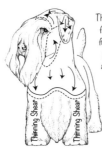

The head is long and rectangular with a fall of hair between the eyes. From the front and rear, the legs drop in straight, parallel lines from well-toned shoulders and thighs. When setting the pattern, use the turn of the muscles to set the lines. Under the tail is short and clean with a drape of longer fur covering the back of the thighs. Leg furnishings are longer than the body coat.

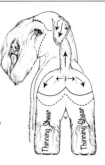

Thinning Shear

Thinning Shear

Soft Coated Wheaton Terrier CURLY & WAVY COATED

Breed Facts & Characteristics

Country of Origin: *Ireland*

Height at Shoulder: *17"–19"*

Coat Length/Type: *Long/Soft*

Color: *Always a yellow wheaten with darker gray shadowing allowed in the facial area.*

Correct grooming procedure:
Hand-Scissor

Common pet grooming practices:
Clipper-Trim

-The Goal-
Breed outline is square with enough coat to float with the dog as it moves. Head is well covered with fur and rectangular in shape. All pattern lines are invisible. Mat free.

Head is rectangular with a fall over the eyes and a long beard.

Ear is clipped at the fold.

Correctly Groomed: Hand-Scissored

Typical blades used for pet grooming range from a #4F blade to a variety of guard combs in a combination of lengths.

Clip sanitary areas.

Rump is tight and clean showing off a well angulated rear assembly with strong thighs.

Throat is short and the chest is flat.

Pattern lines are well blended.

BLENDING AREA

Hocks are well let down.

Legs are scissored full, straight and parallel.

Underline is short and tailored. Depth of chest to the elbow.

Scissor

Scissor

Trim nails as short as possible or grind.

Feet are tight and round.

General Description

The Wheaten is a medium sized, squarely built, robust dog with a great sense of humor and responsiveness to its surroundings. Has a rectangular head style and compact body with a deep chest. Silky, profuse hair falls in soft waves and is considered single coated. Color is always a yellow wheaten with darker gray shadowing allowed in facial area.

Head Study Soft Coated Wheaton Terrier

Their expression is friendly, active and self-confident. Head is rectangular with a long fall of hair over the stop area with a full beard. The top skull and the muzzle are equal in length with the stop area being the center point. All lines on the head are soft and blended.

Clip top skull with a range of medium to longer guard combs pulled forward from the occiput and feathering off at the fall area.

Line for the fall follows eye socket rim. Back corners of eyes are trimmed with thinning shears, slightly exposing the eye.

On muzzle, hair is long and natural but does not break the line of the top skull. When combing down beard, lines at the side of the face form a straight plane. Just below back corner of the eyes, fur is short and well blended, creating fill under the eye. Beard clipper lines are soft and blended.

When setting beard, use back corners of the eyes and whisker nodule on cheeks and under jaw as basic guidelines. "Connect the dots."

This ear is more coated than other terriers. Work from the center of the ear out with a #7F, #5F or a #4F blade on the outside of the ear. A #40 blade can be used on the inside of the ear leather with a very light touch. Start the clipper work at the fold, not the base of the ear. The fold of the ear is level with the line of the top skull. Edge the ear with small detailing shears.

Ear Safety Tip:
Remember, always keep tips of the shears towards the tips of the ears when edging for safety.

Blend Well

Transitional Blending Area

Blend Well

Throat is trimmed with blades ranging from a #4F to a #5F, or short to medium guard combs, with the lay of the coat.

Stay inside the neck's natural cowlick line that runs from ear bulb down in a "U" or "V" shape. Stop about 3 or 4 finger widths above the breast bone. Thinning shear the cowlick seam to blend with the longer coat of the neck.

From the front and rear, the legs drop in straight, parallel lines from well-toned shoulders and thighs. When setting the pattern, use the turn of the muscles to set the lines. Chest is flat but use caution not to bald out this area due to cowlicks where the front legs join the chest. Rear is short, tight and clean. Leg furnishings are longer than the body coat.

Scissor Scissor Scissor

Scissor Scissor

Breed Facts & Characteristics

Country of Origin: *Italy*

Height at Shoulder: *22"–27"*

Coat Length/Type: *Hard/Wiry*

Color: *All white or white with tan, rust or brown areas.*

Correct grooming procedure:
Card & Hand-Strip

Common pet grooming practices:
Hand-Strip

-The Goal-
Looks more like a hound than a pointer. Coat should be hard, a bit rough and wiry. Hand-stripping is the only way to retain proper coat texture, which protects the skin while working in the field.

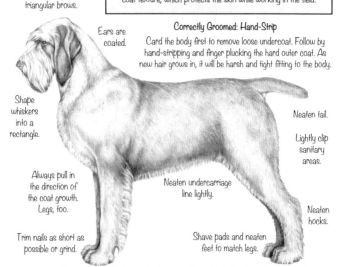

Top of skull and cheek area very tight. Clear between eyes. Split, medium sized, triangular brows.

Ears are coated.

Correctly Groomed: Hand-Strip
Card the body first to remove loose undercoat. Follow by hand-stripping and finger plucking the hard outer coat. As new hair grows in, it will be harsh and tight fitting to the body.

Shape whiskers into a rectangle.

Neaten tail.

Lightly clip sanitary areas.

Always pull in the direction of the coat growth. Legs, too.

Neaten undercarriage line lightly.

Neaten hocks.

Trim nails as short as possible or grind.

Shave pads and neaten feet to match legs.

The coat should look as natural as possible and be 1–2 inches all over the body.

General Description

A tough, slow, and methodical all-purpose hunting dog of moderate size. The head is somewhat rectangular and accentuated by a harsh-coated beard. Eyes are set off by shaggy eyebrows. Coat is made up of a wiry, harsh outer coat with a thick under coat that is heavier in the winter and almost non-existent in the summer. The harsh outer coat is normally short and rough. Ideally the dog is covered with coat ranging between 1 and 3 inches.

The top of the head from behind the eyebrows to the base of the skull is stripped tight and close. Blend at occiput/neck junction.

Shape longer triangular type eyebrows with thinning shears.

Do not totally clear the stop area. A fan of hair should be left in front of the eyes.

The beard should be longer. Use thinners to create a natural rectangular shape balancing with the rest of the dog.

Hand-strip or thinning shear the longer hair on the ear leather. Edge with thinners for a natural look.

Neaten throat area to the breast bone. Tidy cowlick ridge on sides of neck with thinners.

Ear Safety Tip:
Remember, always keep the tips of the shears towards the tips of the ears when edging for safety.

The Spinone does not have a distinct pattern. They look very "natural" when finished. The coat should be carded and hand-stripped or "rolled" every few months to maintain its harsh texture. On the body and legs, the coat should be between 1–2 inches in length. The top of the head from back of the eyebrows to the base of the skull is shorter. The throat area is also shorter. Tidy the "fan" in the stop area slightly with thinners. Trim pads but leave coat on the foot more natural.

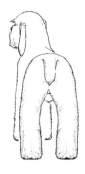

Breed Facts & Characteristics

Country of Origin: *Germany*

Height at Shoulder: *17½"–19½"*

Coat Length/Type: *Hard/Wiry*

Color: *Salt and pepper or black.*

Correct grooming procedure:
Hand-Strip

Common pet grooming practices:
Clipper-Trim

-The Goal-
This is a tight and very tailored-looking dog. The body is almost square in build with a rectangular head. When finished, pattern lines are invisible.

~Head Shape ~
Strong & Rectangular

Brows are long, arched triangles exposing a keen eye expression.

Ears trimmed very close.

~Pet Clipper-Trim~
Blade choices for the bulk of the body range from a #10 to a #4F. Longer blade choices can be used in reverse for closer, super smooth results.

Beard is left long and natural.

"Card" clippered body area to help promote proper coat growth and retain color.

Use natural cowlick line to set neck pattern.

Show off a powerful rear by accentuating a well angulated hind-end. Use the thigh muscle to set the pattern line.

BLENDING AREA

Chest is flat from profile. Watch for cowlicks.

Slight rise into the tuck-up area.

Brisket to elbow.

Lowest point of pattern should be at bend.

Legs fall in parallel lines from the shoulder. Use the shoulder muscle to set pattern line.

Scissor legs into columns.

Round feet.

Hocks are well let down.

Feet are rounded and face straight forward.

Pads are trimmed close.

General Description

The Standard Schnauzer is a powerful, muscular and squarely built dog of high energy and great intelligence. Its tail is docked short. It may have cropped or uncropped ears. When grooming, remember there is nothing soft or fluffy about the breed. In the finished groom, there is very little coat hiding the contours of its body. Leg coat and muzzle coat are slightly longer. Breed hallmarks are rectangular head, arched eyebrows and full mustache and beard.

Head Study — Standard Schnauzer

Shape the arched eyebrows by following the eye socket ridge. Stop area is clear, creating split brows. Use curved shears in reverse to help shape the eyebrows. The coat is very short at the back of the eye and gets longer towards the nose. Brows tips reach to the halfway point of the muzzle.

Hand-strip or clipper the top skull very close. If clipping, use blades ranging from a #10 used with the grain to a #4F used against the grain, depending on the coat density.

The ears may be cropped or natural. Either type is clipper-trimmed very close with blades ranging from a #10 or #15 on the outside and a #40 on the inside. Finish by edging the ears with small detailing shears.

The beard and mustache form a rectangular head style. When viewed straight on, the cheeks and the beard should form one continuous line.

The occiput is the dividing line between the head and the neck.

The cheeks and throat are smooth and clean. Blades ranging from a #10 to a #15, used with or against the grain, are common in pet styling. The line runs from the back corner of the eye to the cheek whisker nodule, to the chin nodule, up to the opposite cheek whisker nodule and opposite eye. Use the zygomatic arch to set the line from the back corner of the eye to the ear canal. The natural cowlick line assists with setting the throat area. Create a soft "V" or "U" shape coming about 3–4 finger widths above the breast bone.

Ear Safety Tip:
Remember, always keep the tips of the shears towards the tips of the ears when edging for safety.

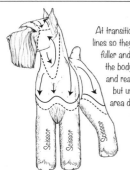

At transition points on the body, blend the lines so they are invisible. Legs should be left fuller and fall into straight columns, from the body to the feet, on both the front and rear legs. The chest should be flat but use caution not to bald out this area due to cowlicks found where the front legs meet the chest.

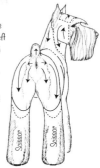

Breed Facts & Characteristics

Country of Origin: *Wales*

Height at Shoulder: *14"–15½"*

Coat Length/Type: *Hard/Wiry*

Color: *Black and tan (black saddle, tan flatwork and furnishings).*

Correct grooming procedure:
Hand-Strip

Common pet grooming practices:
Clipper-Trim

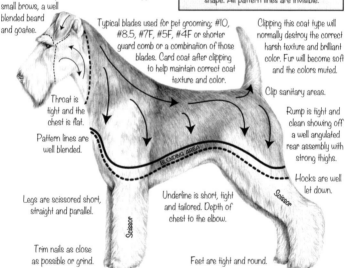

-The Goal-
Everything about this breed is tight and tailored. The well-toned body is accentuated by the groom. The head is rectangular in shape. All pattern lines are invisible.

Correctly Groomed:
Hand-Stripped

Head is brick shaped with small brows, a well blended beard and goatee.

Typical blades used for pet grooming; #10, #8.5, #7F, #5F, #4F or shorter guard comb or a combination of those blades. Card coat after clipping to help maintain correct coat texture and color.

Clipping this coat type will normally destroy the correct harsh texture and brilliant color. Fur will become soft and the colors muted.

Throat is tight and the chest is flat.

Clip sanitary areas.

Rump is tight and clean showing off a well angulated rear assembly with strong thighs.

Pattern lines are well blended.

BLENDING AREA

Hocks are well let down.

Legs are scissored short, straight and parallel.

Underline is short, tight and tailored. Depth of chest to the elbow.

Scissor

Scissor

Trim nails as close as possible or grind.

Feet are tight and round.

General Description

Everything about the Welsh Terrier is tight and tailored. This is a squarely built dog of medium size. He is hardy and sturdy, yet extremely agile. When grooming this breed, remember there is nothing soft or fluffy about it. In the finished groom, there is very little coat hiding the contours of its body. The leg coat is slightly longer. The head is rectangular in shape with a piercing expression, moderate muzzle coat and small brows.

Head is brick shaped with small brows and a well blended beard and goatee. Expression is friendly but alert and bold. The top skull and muzzle are equal in length with the stop area being the center point. All lines on head are invisible.

The eyebrows are very small, split at the stop area. There are no sharp lines. Shape and blend with thinning shears.

On the muzzle, the hair is longer but not so long as to extend beyond the planes of the top skull or cheeks. Blend the bulk of the muzzle with thinning shears or skim with a medium guard comb. Lightly trim the end of the muzzle to accentuate the rectangular head style. The lines at the side of the face are well blended and straight. Do not hollow out under the eye.

Blend Well

Blend Well

Blend Well

Blend Well

Transitional Blending Area

The throat is trimmed close with a #7F used against the grain or a #10 or #15 blade used with the coat growth.

Clip top skull with blades ranging from a #7F to a #5F, with the grain.

Use a #10 or #15 blade on the outside of the ear. A #40 blade can be used on the inside of the ear leather with a very light touch. Edge the ear with small detailing shears. The fold of the ear comes to just above the line of the top skull.

Ear Safety Tip:
Remember, always keep the tips of the shears towards the tips of the ears when edging for safety.

Stay inside the neck's natural cowlick line that runs from ear bulb down in a "U" or "V" shape. Stop about 2 or 3 finger widths above breast bone. Thinning shear the cowlick seam to blend with longer coat of the neck.

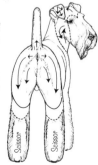

From the front and rear, the legs drop in straight, parallel lines from well-toned shoulders and thighs. When setting the pattern, use the turn of the muscles to set the lines. Chest is flat but use caution not to bald out this area due to cowlicks where the front legs join the chest. Rear is short, tight and clean. Leg furnishings are slightly longer than the body coat.

Scissor

Scissor

Scissor

Scissor

Scissor

West Highland White Terrier

WIRE COATED

Breed Facts & Characteristics

Country of Origin: *Scotland*

Height at Shoulder: *10"–11"*

Coat Length/Type: *Hard/Wiry*

Color: *White only.*

Correct grooming procedure:
Hand-Strip

Common pet grooming practices:
Clipper-Trim

> -The Goal-
> Everything about this breed is compact and tailored. Muscular body is
> accentuated by the groom. Head is full and round with eyes and nose
> in the center of the head piece. Pattern lines on body are invisible.

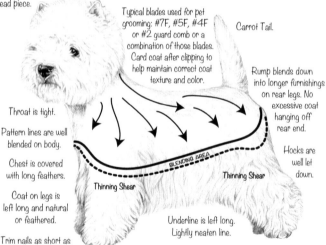

Head is full and round. Eyes and nose are centered in the head piece.

Top ⅓ of ear tip is clipped.

Correctly Groomed: Hand-Strip

Typical blades used for pet grooming: #7F, #5F, #4F or #2 guard comb or a combination of those blades. Card coat after clipping to help maintain correct coat texture and color.

Carrot Tail.

Rump blends down into longer furnishings on rear legs. No excessive coat hanging off rear end.

Throat is tight.

Pattern lines are well blended on body.

Chest is covered with long feathers.

Coat on legs is left long and natural or feathered.

Trim nails as short as possible or grind.

BLENDING AREA

Thinning Shear

Thinning Shear

Hocks are well let down.

Underline is left long. Lightly neaten line.

Feet are rounded. Front are feet larger than rear feet.

General Description

This is a resilient little dog with great strength and agility. The top section shows off a toned body while the lower section is feathered. The head is round in shape, accentuated by dark, piercing eyes and small erect ears that peek out above the coat on top of the head. The expression is piercing, full of purpose and vigor.

Their expression is friendly, inquisitive and bold. Head is full and round. The ears are small, triangular and erect. The eyes are deep set. When viewed from the front, the eyes and nose are at the center of a well-balanced circle. When finished, the head is well blended and soft.

Pull the hair up, trimming the coat on the top of the head, to just below level with the ear tips using thinning shears.

Comb fur forward, over the brows. With curved shears in reverse, trim a frame around eye area. The line is beveled with a deep set eye. Finish by softening the line with thinning shears.

Trim stop area lightly with thinning shears before framing eye area.

Lower line of the head completes the circle that puts the eyes and nose at the center of the head piece when looking from the front. Lower line parallels jaw bone. Comb all the coat down and trim with shears in a curved line running from the nose all the way up to behind the occiput. Soften line with thinning shears to complete head piece.

The top ⅓ of the ear tip is clipped. Use a # 10 or #15 blade on the outside of the ear. A #40 blade can be used on the inside of the ear leather with a very light touch. Edge ear with small detailing shears.

Ear Safety Tip: Remember, always keep tips of shears towards tips of the ears when edging for safety.

The line at the back of the skull is about an inch beyond the occiput.

The throat is clipped with a blade slightly shorter than that used on the body, in a "U" shape, about 2–3 finger widths from the breast bone.

The head is round and full with eyes and nose at the center. From the front and rear, the legs drop in straight, parallel lines from well-toned shoulders and thighs. When setting the pattern, use the turn of the muscles to set the lines. Under the tail is short and clean with a drape of longer fur covering the back of the thighs. Leg furnishings are longer than the body coat. Tail is carrot shaped and very short on the back side.

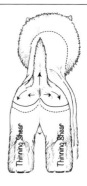

Breed Facts & Characteristics

Country of Origin: *Holland*

Height at Shoulder: *20"-24"*

Coat Length/Type: *Moderate/Wiry*

Color: *Their base color is grizzled gray with strong liver color tones coming through the coat.*

Correct grooming procedure:
Hand-Strip

Common pet grooming practices:
Hand-Strip, Bathe & Brush Out

-The Goal-
Hallmark of the breed is the coat. It is a double coat; topcoat is harsh wiry, medium length and straight. Undercoat is thick and dense. The dog should appear somewhat rough and untidy but clean.

Lightly hand-strip the top of the head, the ears and the cheeks.

Eyebrows are full and triangular in shape.

Brush with a firm slicker brush to remove dead coat and tangles. Finger pluck harsh outer jacket to neaten slightly.

Neaten tail to match body.

If shedding, card coat to remove loose undercoat.

Neaten hocks.

Typically, the legs are covered with shorter and softer coat than found on the body.

Neaten undercarriage line lightly.

Lightly clip sanitary areas: Under tail and tummy if needed with a #10.

Trim nails as short as possible or grind.

Shave pads and neaten feet to match legs.

General Description

The Wirehaired Pointing Griffon is a tough, all-purpose hunting dog of moderate size. The breed has great stamina and excels in wet, swampy terrain. The distinctive coat is made up of a wiry, harsh outer coat with a thick under coat that is heavier in the winter and almost non-existent in the summer. The harsh, outer guard coat is normally between 1"–2" in length and never trimmed, giving the breed a shaggy, rough appearance. The extended "eyebrows" and typical beard give this dog his characteristic appearance.

On the top of the head, card out dead undercoat with a fine stripping knife or carding tool. Hand-strip or finger pluck the longer hair.

Hand-strip the longer hair on the ear leather. Edge the ear with small shears or thinning shears for a very natural look.

Leave eye brows, coat in the stop area and muzzle coat natural

The hallmarks of this breed are their full eyebrows, beards and moustaches. These areas are to be left full and natural.

Ear Safety Tip:
Remember, always keep the tips of the shears towards the tips of the ears when edging for safety.

The Griffon is not "groomed" into a style or pattern however the shaggy coat does need to be hand-stripped or "rolled" every few months to maintain it's harsh texture. Use an undercoat rake, carding tool or stripping knife to consistently work over the entire dog, removing blown undercoat. Feet, hocks and under the tail can be tidied up with shears or thinning shears.

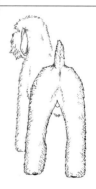

Drop Coat Breeds

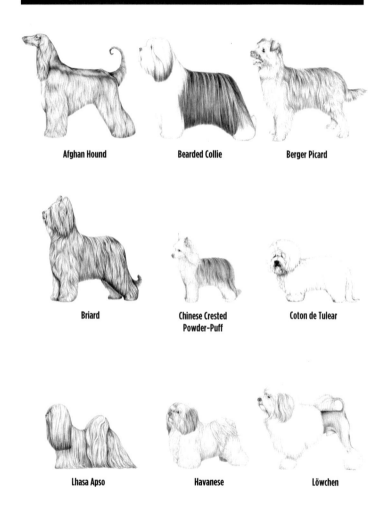

Afghan Hound

Bearded Collie

Berger Picard

Briard

Chinese Crested
Powder-Puff

Coton de Tulear

Lhasa Apso

Havanese

Löwchen

Drop Coat Breeds

Maltese

Old English Sheepdog

Polish Lowland Sheepdog

Pyrenean Shepherd

Silky Terrier

Shih Tzu

Skye Terrier

Tibetan Terrier

Yorkshire Terrier

Left in it's natural state, this coat type will grow very long, almost dropping to the ground on many breeds. This hair type is considered non-shedding. For many of the breeds, groomed-to-breed standard, long coats are left in natural state, with very little trimming. The coat has a tendency to form mats and tangles if not brushed regularly —at least three times weekly—or unless the dog is kept in a low maintenance trim style. If not properly cared for, mats and tangles may make shaving coat and starting over the only humane alternative.

Correct head styles from breed to breed vary including tied-up top-knots, buttons, braids, minor trimming or left with a natural veil shielding the dog's eyes. In a pet situation, most owners prefer to see the eyes of their beloved pet.

Natural Coat: Fully Brushed Out

-The Goal-
Coat should be mat- and tangle-free.
The fur should be light and airy, moving
freely with the dog as it moves.

Topknot is either left loose or braided
with two braids, one over each eye.

Clear stop
area with
thinners or
clippers.

Leave ears
long.

Line comb and brush every inch of
this dog, right down to the skin.

Lightly trim
sanitary
area—both
under tail and
tummy.

Watch friction areas:
• Collar Area
• Arm Pits
• Behind Ears
• Legs & Thighs

Trim nails as short as
possible or grind.

Shave pads and scissor
feet round. Neaten
undercarriage line lightly.

The common denominator of a "drop coat" is fine, straight hair texture. If you comb the coat up or fluff it out, it has a natural tendency to drop back towards the ground. Typical breeds with this coat type include Shih Tzus, Lhasas, Maltese or any pets of similar coat type, purebred or mixed breed. The look, style and variety of even the most simple trims can be astounding. The style will be influenced by the physical appearance of the dog—body structure, ear and tail type, coat texture, color and the overall length of trim. Styling options for head, ears and tail are truly varied, limited only by the pet stylist's abilities, pet owner's discretion and the pet's lifestyle. A knowledgeable and talented pet stylist can impart style and flair to any trim option, creating an adorable haircut style for the pet.

Stylized Trim

For trims using a shorter blade on the body, use the higher blending line near the tail as a transitional line. Change to a medium or longer guard comb to set the rump. If using a longer guard comb on the body, follow   through to the blending areas and   feather off.

-The Goal-
The dog should look soft and cuddly, like a small stuffed animal. The coat is smooth and even without any scissor or clipper marks. Head, ear and tail styles can vary based on client preference.

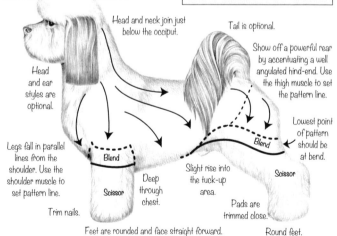

Head and neck join just below the occiput.

Tail is optional.

Show off a powerful rear by accentuating a well angulated hind-end. Use the thigh muscle to set the pattern line.

Head and ear styles are optional.

Lowest point of pattern should be at bend.

Blend

Legs fall in parallel lines from the shoulder. Use the shoulder muscle to set pattern line.

Blend

Scissor

Deep through chest.

Slight rise into the tuck-up area.

Scissor

Pads are trimmed close.

Trim nails.

Feet are rounded and face straight forward.

Round feet.

For a fuller round head style, pull a medium or longer guard comb forward from the occiput toward the eyes.

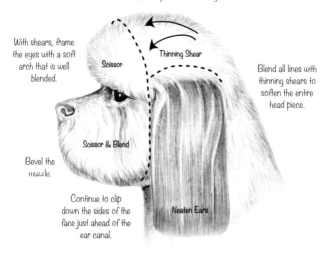

With shears, frame the eyes with a soft arch that is well blended.

Scissor

Thinning Shear

Blend all lines with thinning shears to soften the entire head piece.

Scissor & Blend

Bevel the muzzle.

Continue to clip down the sides of the face just ahead of the ear canal.

Neaten Ears

Scissor

Scissor

The eyes and nose are well-balanced in the round head piece. At transition points between the body and the legs, blend the lines so they are invisible. The legs should fall into straight columns, from the body to the rounded feet, when viewed from the front or rear. There are no breaks in the pattern anywhere on the dog.

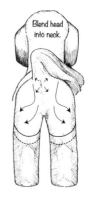

Blend head into neck.

All round heads should have the nose and eyes placed in the center of the circle.
On some drop coated breeds, elongating the muzzle is a stylish alternative.

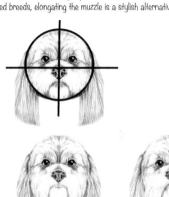

Ears

Shaved or Teddy

Short

Medium

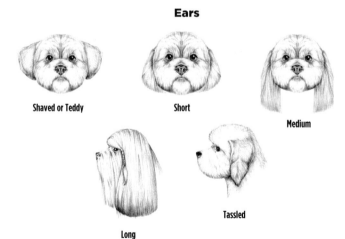

Long

Tassled

Drop Coat Styles Topknots

**Always double check no skin has been caught up into the bands by sliding
the teeth of a comb between the band(s) and the skin.**

Single Tie-Up

Single tied up topknots can
be pulled up as one ponytail
or two ponytails that are
combined with a third band.

Tie-Up with Buttons

Two button topknots pulled up
the center of the head.

To keep the button neat after it
is formed, minimize handling the
button when applying bows.

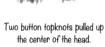
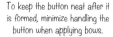

Squirrel
This tail style leaves the coat between
½ to 2 inches in overall length.

Blunt Cut
Trimming the tail straight across in a neat
fashion offers a low maintenance style
while retaining some length.

Plumed
Brush tail and hold tail over the back in its natural carriage. With
thinners or shears, nip some "V" shaped cuts into the fur, paralleling
the strands of hair as they hang. The "V" nips can be between 1"
and 3" depending on how munch length needs to be removed.

Natural
Brush the tail thoroughly and
leave untrimmed.

Lion
Using same blade used on body, continue the
clipper work out onto the tail. Clip to within
⅓ to ⅔ of the base of the tailbone, leaving a
natural plume on the end.